Positive I

The Positive Behavior Principles make so much sense. Dan speaks in such a way that leaves you excited, nodding your head "yes" constantly, and wondering why you didn't figure all of this out yourself. I highly recommend Dan's work for its relatability, ease of reading, and great sense of humor in the midst of making connections and discoveries.

Malia Huffman, Counselor
Cloverdale, Virginia

Adopting these principles shifted my approach to classroom management, and as my perspective changed, so did my outcomes. Rather than expecting compliance with my policies and systems, I began connecting with individual students and strengthening relationships. In the most challenging situations, I no longer expect too much at once. I start with one or two small, concrete target behaviors and build on successes. These principles have given me strategies that have worked and have resulted in transformation in my classroom.

Elizabeth McLeod, Teacher
Monterey, California

As a seasoned educator and now, an instructional coach, I find the strategies and techniques in this body of work to be a significant shift from how we, as veteran teachers, were once taught to address behavioral challenges. Classrooms move from a place of rules and consequences to engaging communities filled with choice and rigorous achievement grounded in meaningful relationships. I have become a huge advocate for the message and meaning behind the *Positive Behavior Principles* and have watched them transform the way teachers teach and learners learn.

Barbara D'Leise Triplett, Instructional Coach
San Antonio, Texas

Dan has worked with teachers in my former and current districts over the course of the past five years implementing the Positive Behavior Principles, and our students have derived a great deal of benefit from learning from teachers who build strong relationships with them and who understand the value of teaching skills that help our students make better behavioral choices each day.

Dr. Daniel Loughran, Assistant Superintendent
Franklin, New Jersey

Praise for
Positive Behavior Principles

Our paradigm in education, when students misbehave, has been consequences and punishments such as detentions, suspensions, and even expulsions, with little success. Dan's body of work teaches us that our paradigm needs to shift so the messages we send to kids are that we want them in school and think they are worth the time and effort, and through the relationship, they will want to do better and so will we.

Dr. Jean Anderson, Special Education Director
Kearney, Nebraska

Dan's language around behavior has become engrained in our school culture, making it easy for me, as well as teachers and support staff, to communicate with children using the same language and expectations for our students. The Positive Behavior Principles have helped our staff change deep-seated beliefs and practices that no longer serve them or their students well.

Brandee Sabala, Principal
Gooding, Idaho

The focus on positive principles for behavior management and changing the way we view behavior not just in children, but adults as well, is such a game changer for how educators manage discipline. I now believe children who come into my classroom with the most difficult challenges are lacking skills to manage their own behaviors, and that I can help them through teaching lessons on self-regulation. This body of work has truly inspired me to become a better teacher.

Amanda Hawes, Teacher
Aransas Pass, Texas

In seeking to create a school-wide, multi-tiered system of support for behavior, it can be challenging to wade through the gamut of evidence-based "programs" and "strategies." This book, however, breaks down each tier of intervention, clearly spelling out instructional strategies that can be successful regardless of whether or not the school has adopted a particular program.

Liz Meredith, EdD, Director of Curriculum and Instruction
Byesville, Ohio

Duplication and Copyright

NCYI titles may be purchased in bulk at special discounts for educational, business, fundraising, or promotional use. For more information, please email sales@ncyi.org.

NATIONAL CENTER for
YOUTH ISSUES

P.O. Box 22185 • Chattanooga, TN 37422-2185
423-899-5714 • 866-318-6294 • fax: 423-899-4547
www.ncyi.org

ISBN: 9781937870713
E-book: 9781953945365
Library of Congress Control Number: 2020908322
© 2020 National Center for Youth Issues, Chattanooga, TN
All rights reserved.

Written by: Dan St. Romain
Published by National Center for Youth Issues

Printed at Starkey Printing • Chattanooga, TN, U.S.A.
January 2022

POSITIVE
Behavior
Principles

Shifting Perspectives and Aligning Practices in Schools

Published by

NATIONAL CENTER for
YOUTH ISSUES

Contents

Introduction

"I just want to teach. Is that too much to ask?" This was the sentiment of a new high school teacher I was coaching. At the time, I had just started working at our regional education service center, and as part of my new duties, I was charged with going into schools and providing consultative behavior support to teachers. Needless to say, there was no shortage of work for me. "I went into education because I love math," the teacher told me. "When I went through school, one of my teachers instilled in me a love for math, and I just want to pass that love on to my students, but I can't, because I spend all of my time dealing with behavior problems." After observing her class, I agreed.

This was not the first time I had heard some version of this story. I felt overwhelmed and at a loss for what to say. After providing her a few strategies, I wished her luck, told her I would pray for her, and went on my way. I spent that entire week going from class to class, putting out one fire, only to have another one pop up somewhere else. *Is that it?* I thought. *Strategies, luck, and prayer?* I knew something had to change.

I was one of three behavior consultants offering support in the region, and our job seemed unrealistic. Fortunately, around this same time, my colleagues and I were exposed to a body of work by George Sugai, a researcher from the University of Connecticut, called Positive Behavior Support, as well as training in the Boys Town Education Model (BTEM). Both models emphasized taking a prosocial approach to behavior management, using discipline as an opportunity to teach positive behaviors. The information intrigued me enough to dive in at a much deeper level.

Because the regional needs outweighed the amount of support the three of us were able to provide, my coworkers and I designed the ABC Program. As a way of **A**ddressing **B**ehavioral **C**oncerns, we worked with fifty individuals around the region over the course of three years to certify them as behavioral consultants for their school districts. In the first year of the program, we focused on aligning behavioral beliefs. The second year was spent providing the candidates with strategies for offering consultations and presentations, and during the final year, each of the participants had to revamp the discipline efforts at their school, creating alternatives to traditional punishment-based interventions such as in-school suspension (ISS) and detention. Instead, they designed intervention methods based on the teaching of social skills.

This three-year period was transformational for me. Although we designed the program for the regional participants, I learned just as much in my supervisory role. My perspective on behavior shifted and was solidified. I was able to move away from believing in a model of traditional rewards and punishments toward one of teaching. By the end of the program, I felt as though I understood what seemed to work, why it worked, and what needed to be done to move our discipline efforts forward.

Shortly thereafter I was hired as a behavior consultant for a school district, and over the course of the following decade I split my time between working directly with students on behavior issues and providing consultation and staff development for teachers. It was during this time that my body of work seemed to unfold, both in theory and practice.

While going into classrooms to offer support, I saw themes emerged. I discovered that behavior concerns teachers faced seemed to be due to one of the following reasons:

- Instructional Problems: Students misbehaving because they were not engaged in learning
- Modeling: Staff members inadvertently reinforcing negative behaviors through modeling
- Attention Issues: Teachers reinforcing negative behaviors by drawing attention to them
- Crisis Intervention: Staff members getting into power struggles with students
- Relationships: Students not connecting with staff
- Punishment-Based Models: Failed interventions based on negative reinforcement

I found myself offering the same set of suggestions, based on these core issues, the result of which developed into this body of work: Positive Behavior Principles.

Since that time, I have worked with countless schools and teachers, implementing this body of work in their schools. Although I have received a great deal of positive feedback on how this information has helped teachers implement successful strategies in their classroom, I believe the greatest benefit of the principles is one of alignment. Teachers will have a hard time finding success with strategies if they don't align the strategies with their beliefs. And that is what led me to write this book. *Positive Behavior Principles* helps individual teachers, as well as entire schools, align their strategies with their beliefs.

This information is not a program, nor is it a one-size-fits-all set of strategies. It is a framework for helping educators analyze their behavioral perspectives and practices. Teacher strategies should be individualized and will change based on a variety of factors—grade levels, teaching styles, settings, personalities, etc. What works for one teacher might not work for another, but what should remain constant is the philosophy on which the strategies are based. The nine Positive Behavior Principles, at their core, outline a set of beliefs based on a prosocial approach to discipline management:

1. Healthy relationships positively influence student behaviors.

2. Instructional practices impact behaviors.

3. If students' basic needs are not met, behavior concerns will surface.

4. Educators should model expected behaviors.

5. Attention is a powerful tool for shaping behavior.

6. Students' social and emotional developmental levels should be considered when determining interventions.

7. Discipline efforts should be rooted in the practice of teaching and reinforcing behavioral skills.

8. When students are overly stressed, they are not open to behavioral instruction. De-escalation should be the primary concern.

9. Behaviors are not always the result of choice. Habits, as well as a variety of other factors, trigger behaviors. These reasons should be considered when designing interventions.

These beliefs make a great filter through which educators can analyze their practices. I have worked with countless administrators and teachers, implementing this body of work in their schools. And although I have received a great deal of positive feedback on how this information has helped individual teachers implement successful strategies in their classroom, I believe the greatest benefit of the principles is one of alignment. Positive Behavior Principles help teachers, as well as entire schools, align perspectives and implement successful behavioral strategies that work.

Positive Behavior Principles help teachers, as well as entire schools, align perspectives and implement successful behavioral strategies that work.

Positive Behavior Support

The nine Positive Behavior Principles were designed to complement the Positive Behavior Support (PBS) model (now referred to as Positive Behavior Interventions and Supports, or PBIS) which gained momentum in the late 1990s.[1] This approach is not a specific program, but rather a general framework for improving student behaviors using proactive, positive, and systematic methods.

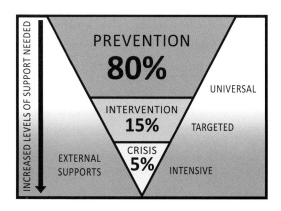

The PBS triangle outlines three levels of behavioral support needed in schools. At the top of the triangle universal strategies are designed for prevention. Examples include outlining expectations, having consistent routines, and acknowledging positive choices. Though universal strategies are afforded to all students, approximately 80 percent of students in a given setting will be successful with this level of support. Moving down the triangle, roughly 15 percent of students will need additional targeted interventions. Examples could include participation in a social skill group, visual cues, and preferential seating. Despite prevention and intervention efforts, about 5 percent of students need ongoing intensive support due to the severity of their behaviors falling into a level of crisis. Individualized plans are usually needed for this group of students.

The triangle can be likened to a sieve with supports and interventions at each level. When students are unsuccessful at one level, they drop through to the next level where more interventions are afforded. The lower the students go, the more their internal control often decreases, increasing the number of external behavioral supports needed to be successful.

In each of the three sections of the triangle, Positive Behavior Principles are outlined for consideration at that level of support. Although all principles can be utilized at all levels, they should receive special consideration at the level they are outlined. For example, the seventh principle emphasizes the importance of teaching specific behavioral skills. Although all students should receive proactive social skill instruction, targeted behavioral skill development should be one of the main interventions for students with greater behavior concerns. Also, each section builds on prior sections. For example, the first principle outlines the importance of relationship building. Although this principle is in the first of the three sections, it is the foundation for all principles and, thus, critical at all levels.

Pick a Student–Any Student

As noted, one of the main goals of this book is to help educators align behavioral perspectives with practices. Although I hope readers have many aha moments while reading, this book is also meant to provide educators with practical classroom strategies. My guess is that if you are reading this, you have students who need high levels of behavioral support. In order to make the most of the information outlined, I recommend picking one of your students to focus on as you read. Think about the implications of each principle and accompanying strategies for that student. By doing so, you are more likely to focus on specific strategies to try, which will increase the chance of theory turning into good practice.

—Dan St. Romain

Prevention Principles

The first four principles are designed to prevent misbehavior and help educators align their philosophy and strategies. When teachers build strong relationships with students, incorporate multimodal teaching strategies, and model healthy behaviors, they provide a strong foundation for good behavior in schools. However, if these practices are not in place, the 80 percent of students who would typically demonstrate appropriate behaviors might have difficulty doing so in these settings.

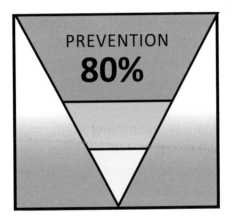

1. Behavior mainly occurs in a **relationship**.

   Our interactions with others shape our behaviors, as visually represented by the shaking hands icon. Rather than trying to focus on student behaviors, or ours, the best strategy is to examine the individual interactions that shape our relationships. When we change the dynamic of our relationships, we will change the behaviors.

2. Effective teaching incorporates a balance of **ritual** and **novelty**.

   Teaching practices impact discipline.
   Teachers who have good teaching practices are more likely to have fewer discipline problems. By balancing instructional practices infused with novelty and grounded predictable rituals, we will have a positive impact on behaviors in the classroom. The icon of the scale is designed to represent this balance.

3. It is easier to **channel** behavior than to stop it.

   The icon of the water reminds us that when it comes to behavior, it is far easier to channel it than to try and stop it. When we encourage students to get their talking and moving needs met through multimodal instructional practices, we decrease the chance that they will get those needs met in a way that interrupts teaching and learning in the classroom.

4. **Modeled behaviors** are internalized.

   We are all shaped by our environment. Since behaviors mainly occur in a relationship, student behaviors are influenced by adults. The mirror icon reminds us to be mindful of what we are teaching through our own behaviors. We want to be positive role models for our students.

PREVENTION
80%

PRINCIPLE
ONE

Behavior Mainly Occurs in a Relationship

The Wisdom of the Old and the Innocence of the Young

When I first started working at an early childhood center, I learned a lot about human behavior. Trust me. You can't be around three hundred four- and five-year-old children without being enlightened in some way. Though I was billed as the behavior specialist, I often found myself completely at a loss, not knowing what to do when a student went into tantrum mode. And it certainly didn't help that I was a young father of a child who had his own set of challenging behaviors. I quickly realized that I had a lot to learn. Luckily, experience is a great teacher.

As one of my first school projects, I connected our students with residents from a local assisted living facility. Each class "adopted" a foster grandparent. The project was designed to instill a sense of compassion in the children and help them develop empathy for others. I also knew the residents could teach our students some good lessons as well. I just wasn't expecting to be the *recipient* of one of those lessons.

I vividly remember one particular trip to the assisted living center. It was around the holiday season, so our classes were visiting the facility to sing festive songs to the residents. As was often the case, my job was to shadow one specific student who had behavioral difficulties. And as luck would have it, it had been a difficult morning for Zach. No sooner had the class begun to sing the first song when my special friend got upset and wedged himself behind the piano I was playing—in about a twelve-inch crawl space. I tried to coax him out, but that just seemed to make things worse. His behavior escalated as the program continued, and I'm certain my embarrassment and limit-setting approach weren't helping the situation at all.

As the class left the area, Zach hunkered down, refusing to move. I took a deep breath, knowing my next step was to pry him out from behind the piano. Fortunately for me, one of the wise residents noted my struggles and intervened. "Honey," she said to him. "Can you help me with this contraption? It's my walker. It helps me walk. I can't ever get it open." She smiled. He smiled. "Oh, it looks like somebody lost a tooth. Did the tooth fairy visit you?" she asked. Zach didn't answer, but he did come out from behind the piano to help open the walker before running back to join his class.

I stayed behind to thank the resident and apologize for the child's behavior. She just listened to me and grinned. Upon reflection, I'm certain she knew I didn't have a great deal of experience working with young children. "Oh honey," she said, "I reckon he just doesn't know any better. We all do the best we can. Lord knows I can be just as stubborn. There are times when I'd hide behind that piano too if I could fit. When you get to be my age, you realize the only thing that really matters is relationships. Everything else is just water under the bridge." As she wandered off, I heard her mumble, "Ethel, did you see

that boy? He sure was a cutie, that one." And with that one exchange, that wonderful lady taught me a critical life lesson: positive interactions will always change behavior more effectively than any strict consequence.

My limit-setting method with Zachary did not change his behavior, and it ultimately resulted in a power struggle. The lady with the walker used distraction, and by taking a different approach, she yielded a completely different outcome. By focusing on relationship instead of consequence, she was able to elicit positive behaviors. After having some time to reflect on how this situation had unfolded, I realized there was a similar, related lesson to learn: change the relationship and you will change the behavior.

It Takes Two

Behaviors do not occur in a vacuum. They are most often the result of an interpersonal dance between individuals. Every time a teacher interacts with a student, the dance begins, and the behavioral outcome is dependent on the nature and quality of our interactions. With each interaction, our responses and reactions contribute to the behavioral end result.

We have all had an interpersonal dance go poorly, like my experience with Zach at the nursing home. We talk with a student to discuss inappropriate behaviors; he gets defensive. We redirect and justify, and before long the two of us are in a full-blown power struggle. We metaphorically step on each other's feet . . . push and pull . . . and invariably, the dance ends with injuries.

Using another analogy, think of our interactions like a tennis match. We serve the ball and the student returns it. If a student hits the ball hard, we are likely to return the ball the same way, and vice versa. Likewise, if the ball is returned in a non-aggressive fashion, we most often follow suit. Our plays are dependent on our student's, and our interactions continually change based on the individual plays. Newton summed it up in his third law of motion: for every action, there is an equal and opposite reaction.

I know I am sometimes guilty of placing blame on my students when problems occur. *If he would just . . . . She needs to . . . .* The problem with this line of reasoning is that it places the blame on the student and not on the interaction. I fail to take into consideration what I am contributing to the interactions and, thus, to the behavior problems. Rather than blaming my student or myself, I need to examine our interactions. By looking for specific ways to strengthen these interactions, we take blame out of the equation, increasing the chances that behavior on both sides will improve.
I also find this small shift in perspective helps us all become less frustrated when problems invariably occur.

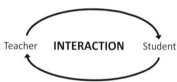

Teacher   **INTERACTION**   Student

Interactions Build Relationships

The sum of our interactions determines the type and quality of our relationships. This can work for or against us. When we have a high number of *positive* interactions with our students, good relationships develop. However, the opposite is true as well. Ongoing *negative* interactions will erode trust and damage our relationships in the process.

Think About It . . .

Pick a few students in your classroom and think about the relationship you have formed with each of them. Now think about your daily interactions. Chances are good that the interactions are positive with those students with whom you have good relationships. However, this isn't always the case with students who exhibit challenging behaviors.

Those Who Need Us Most

Interactions serve as a bridge to build relationships. Unfortunately, some students get very adept at putting up solid barriers, blocking attempts to form healthy relationships. In order to build relationships we have to be willing to be vulnerable, because the truth is, when we connect with others, we run the risk of getting hurt. Some students are not willing—or able—to take this risk because they have been hurt in the past. This is especially the case for students who need higher levels of support in the bottom portions of the PBS triangle.

I have a history of healthy relationships.

It's easy to connect with me.

↑

I have been hurt in the past.

I'm not willing to take
the risk.

Students who are at the top of the triangle are more likely to have a history of healthy relationships. Because they exhibit appropriate behaviors and interactions, they usually have an easier time connecting with others. However, the farther down students fall in this triangle, the more challenging it can be for them to build healthy relationships. Due to their history of behavior problems, they often develop poor interactional habits, which are carried over into new relationships. Their experience with relationships plays out this way:

I take a risk and trust you.

⬇

I exhibit poor behaviors because I am
in the habit of doing so.

⬇

You respond or react in a negative way.

⬇

Your response or reaction triggers more
negative behaviors in me.

⬇

I get hurt.

⬇

I stop trusting.

This pattern plays out with students guarding themselves from getting hurt by sabotaging interactions before healthy relationships even have a chance to develop. Their survival self-talk becomes:

If I don't take a risk and trust you, I won't get hurt.

Like Child, Like Parent

Just as students guard against getting hurt, parents do the same. One teacher told me, "I've been trying to call Kayton's mother, but I can never reach her. I really believe when she sees it is the school's number on her phone, she purposely won't answer the call." I understand this can be frustrating for that teacher, but rather than getting upset with the parent, we should first try to understand why this might be the case.

If parents had a difficult time when *they* were in school, that emotional baggage is carried over into adulthood. They, like children, put up barriers to avoid connecting with school personnel because they don't trust the institution. They might also fear their own children will have similar experiences of failure, and they disconnect, making it difficult for teachers to form relationships.

This situation is exacerbated for parents of children with behavior problems. When parents receive continual negative feedback about their child, they are likely to distance themselves from the school even more. As one parent put it, "Every time I get a note from the school, I dread opening it. I've talked with my son, taken away his phone, and put him on restriction, but he keeps getting in trouble. I'm embarrassed to admit it, but I stopped asking him about his day or checking his folder a long time ago because it always led to more arguing at home. I don't know what else to do."

As this parent shows, frustration and embarrassment often feed the hesitancy to form relationships with school staff. As the parent of a child who had behavior concerns, I can relate. At times I felt helpless, not knowing how to support the teacher. Out of desperation I created distance and didn't work to form relationships. My thought was, "If I don't connect with my son's teachers, it won't be as personal when my son misbehaves and I feel as though I have let them down."

Understanding why students and parents put up barriers to forming relationships does not excuse their behavioral choices. But by understanding the possible reasons for those barriers, we are in a better position to find solutions that result in strengthened relationships.

The Danger of Disconnecting

When students don't form relationships with others and put up walls for self-protection, they have to rely on their own thoughts and beliefs to inform their actions. This is very dangerous for students with behavior problems, as they are at risk for developing very distorted and unhealthy beliefs about their peers and teachers:

If uninterrupted, these thoughts can lead some students to exhibit not only poor, but dangerous behaviors. When we look at the incidents at Virginia Tech, Sandy Hook, Columbine, and other school massacres, we find that many of the perpetrators were loners and had damaged relationships. John Van Dreal, psychologist and director of safety and risk management at Salem-Keizer Public Schools in Oregon, analyzed the reason behind many of these horrific incidents. In looking at the perpetrators, Van Dreal says, "A lot of these people have felt excluded, socially left out or rejected . . . . They don't have any adult connection—no one watching out for them. Or no one knows who they are anymore."[2]

As the number and frequency of dangerous school incidents rises, administrators and legislators continuously look for ways to stop them. Most proposals call for heightened security: locked doors, bulletproof glass, secured visitor entrances, security guards, mesh backpacks, armed staff members, locker searches, etc. Though these strategies might be effective deterrents, they are primarily reactive in nature. Rather than asking, "How do we stop individuals from bringing weapons into the school?" perhaps, a better question would be "Why do students commit these acts in the first place?" I believe the root of the problem stems from damaged relationships. When some students disconnect from others, they can easily develop a me-against-them mentality, which ultimately drives their extreme behaviors.

The Power of Connecting

Healthy relationships are, more often than not, a more effective deterrent against a violent act than any security measure. If students who have committed these atrocities had at least one person in the school with whom they felt connected, these tragedies would have played out very differently. I believe most of the current measures designed to deal with violence in the schools are security Band-Aids, when the real wounds are based in frayed and damaged relationships. Security measures might stop some dangerous incidents from happening in one snapshot of time, but they do nothing to heal the relationships that fueled them in the first place. They also do nothing to alter the distorted perceptions some students have about their peers and school personnel, which is the real issue needing to be confronted.

> *Our goal should be to help children and teens feel motivated to do the right thing out of concern for others rather than fear of punishment.*

When it comes to behavior, one of the most valuable aspects of a relationship is motivation. When we care about people, we are more likely to take into consideration their thoughts and feelings when we make choices. Relationships can serve as a filter, helping us inhibit undesirable behaviors. When we care about a person, we develop empathy. Our goal should be to help children and teens feel motivated to do the right thing out of concern for others rather than fear of punishment. This is more likely to be the case in the context of healthy relationships.

Relationship Building Strategies

It's not always easy to build a relationship with a hurt child, but it is most definitely worth the effort. A healthy student-teacher relationship is the foundation for good behavior in the classroom. Students who trust and respect their teachers will work harder to please them. This is the motivation we want for better behavior in the classroom. In order to build positive relationships, we need positive interactions. When we interact with students, our choices determine whether students put up walls and disconnect from healthy relationships or tear down walls and allow themselves to be vulnerable and connect with us. Here are some strategies for helping them choose healthy connection:

Have Individual Discussions with Students

Interacting with students in a whole group setting is not nearly as impactful or personal as doing so on an individual basis. A teacher can't build individual relationships well in a group setting. This is a problem with large class sizes. The more students in a class, the fewer the individual interactions a teacher can have and the more the quality of those interactions will suffer. You can combat this concern by having individual conversations with students you have identified as being most in need of them. The interactions needn't be long, just individual. This is best accomplished when you can talk with the student alone—in between classes or any time other students are not present. As an added bonus, when you get a student alone, the student will be more apt to let their defenses down, be genuine, and not become clouded by the influence and behaviors of peers.

Talk About Anything but School

Many students, especially those with academic or behavioral challenges, have negative perceptions about school, so when we discuss school-related topics, they shut down. However, when discussing other subjects, such as sporting events or new movies, the school associations don't negatively cloud the interactions and we are able to connect with students on a personal level. We are no longer teachers; we are people. We have all experienced the phenomenon of seeing a student at a restaurant and being greeted with surprise, "I didn't know you ate here!" They are essentially saying, "I've never looked at you as a person, like me, who eats at restaurants. I've always seen you as a teacher. I just thought you lived at school." Talking about non-school related topics helps us strengthen our overall communication and, thus, our relationships with our students.

Find Students' Interests

When we learn about things that are important to our students, we show individual concern. This goes a long way in helping our students feel special for their unique interests. Additionally, when we know what our students like, we are able to build on their interests accordingly. Attending a concert where a student is playing, making content connections based on interests, and commenting on non-school related talents are all ways to validate our students and strengthen our relationships with them in the process.

Acknowledge Individual Attributes and Changes

Students notice when we notice them. When we acknowledge differences or take an interest and comment on differences, we send the message, "I know you well enough to know something is different." This sends the message to the student that we care about their well-being. Simple statements like, "Did you get a haircut over the weekend?" or "You seem upset this morning" go a long way in helping our students feel seen.

Choose to Redirect and Praise Privately

Being called out in public repeatedly can damage relationships. When possible, redirection should be given to students individually through nonverbal signals, eye contact, and private discussions. This is also the case with praise, as some students are embarrassed by public attention. When we call out students in a group setting, we run the risk of embarrassing them. We also set up a good kid/bad kid mindset. The ones who are singled out for positive reasons are the "good kids," and the students who are called out for repeated redirection are the "bad kids." You can avoid this labeling by using individual private interactions as opportunities to provide feedback.

 **PERSPECTIVE** *SHIFT*

If an administrator called you out in a faculty meeting for correction of any type or asked you to stand up repeatedly for praise, my guess is these incidents would make you uncomfortable. You would probably be embarrassed.

The same is true for students. Private individual acknowledgements, both positive and negative, are more effective when given personally.

Connect Students with a Trusted Adult Mentor

Many schools connect students with adult mentors to provide extra support. This is a good strategy; however, too often mentors are chosen *for* students rather than *with* them. By seeking input and determining whom the child most trusts, we are able to build on existing healthy relationships. The stronger the connection students have with their mentors, the more likely the mentors will be able to positively shape the behavior of their mentees. Former teachers, lunch monitors, coaches, counselors, and administrative staff can make great mentors; however, the person's position is not what matters. What matters is finding an individual with whom a student has the most natural connection. When problems arise, it is the person with the best relationship with the student who will most likely be able to broach the incident in a way that will result in a positive change in behavior.

Let Counselors Counsel

Although students, like adults, have a need to connect, some students don't know how to connect. They lack the specific skills to form healthy relationships and need support from school counselors. Unfortunately, many counselors lack the time to offer this support since a great deal of their time is spent carrying out non-counseling duties, such as testing responsibilities, master schedule support, 504 and special education meetings, and so on. Just as we provide tiered support for students struggling academically, we should also provide students with tiered support for behavior. This means priorities need to shift, allowing counselors more time for doing the job for which they were trained—supporting the social and emotional needs of our students.

Put Students in Leadership Roles

When we give students responsibilities, we send the message, "I trust you." This strategy not only serves to strengthen our rapport with students, but it also provides them with a chance to make good choices. Providing students with leadership roles also allows adults collectively to focus on students' strengths.

It is very easy to lose sight of the importance of relationship-building when dealing with difficult behaviors. Sometimes we get so lost in the immediacy of our own needs and frustrations that we fail to remember the long-term goals we are trying to accomplish with students. As a consultant, teachers often say things like, "I don't know why I send Daniel to the office. The administrators don't do anything. In fact, Daniel likes going there."

CAUTION

This is something teachers often tell me about students who are repeatedly sent to the office for misbehavior. After meeting with administrators, I realize the problem is not one of poor strategy; it is a problem of conflicting mindsets. When teachers are looking for a hierarchy of consequences as the means of changing a student's behavior and administrators are focused on relationship-building and creating teachable moments around cause and effect, the result will be frustration for all involved.

I believe administrators focus on relationship-building with students because they understand that disciplining students in the absence of a relationship can often fuel inappropriate behaviors and make things worse. They also know the stronger the connection they have with students, the more receptive the students will be to their interventions.

In Summary . . .

Behaviors almost never occur in isolation. They are impacted by the responses and reactions of others. A student can be placed in several different classrooms and, based on the interactions of the teacher and other students, exhibit very different behaviors in each setting. Analyzing the interplay of these interactions is the first step in creating positive behavior change. When faced with behavioral challenges, a teacher must first ask, "What am I doing to strengthen my relationship with this student?" This is not the only factor impacting the outcome; however, as the connection between the student and teacher improves, the child will be more likely to strive to make positive behavioral choices.

FINAL THOUGHT

One of the most effective ways to create positive behavioral change, be it with students, parents, or colleagues, is to build healthy relationships. When you improve relationships, you improve behaviors.

PRINCIPLE TWO

Effective Teaching Incorporates a Balance of Ritual and Novelty

Not that *Humerus*

"Elvis, Elvis, shakes his . . . pelvis," the students responded in chorus, hands on hips and doing a dance. I'll admit it was a rather alarming statement to hear from a class full of middle school students. "We're late. We're late. We're late for our . . . carpool," they said, tapping their wrists where their watches would be. "Helping us to remember?" asked the teacher. "The carpal bones," the students replied.

At this point I realized the students were reviewing the bones in the body using chants and gestures—and they appeared to be having a great deal of fun doing so. Looking around the room, I saw twenty-two students completely engaged and immersed in learning. This surprised me since the principal asked me to observe this class of students, due to their reputation for being very unruly in their last-period class. Since the students all shared the same daily schedule, I arrived in their prior class period to see how this group handled transitions.

However, I wasn't observing disruptive behaviors in this setting. These teens were laughing and joking, and although the teacher had to provide minor redirection at times, overall the students remained on task and were well-behaved. The problem behaviors I was there to witness weren't evident—at least not in this classroom.

When the bell rang signaling time to transition to their final class, the students did not move, but, instead, watched the teacher intently as she reviewed one last point. "Is your funny bone funny?" she asked. "No! It's humerus," the students responded, pointing to the bones in their upper arms. As they left the class, several kids told the teacher how "punny" she was.

I followed the students to their last class period and introduced myself to the teacher. Upon settling in, I quickly noted a change in the students' behaviors. When the class started, the students continued to have side conversations and talk over the teacher. As questions about content were posed to the group, no one volunteered answers. Though the students had textbooks open, very few appeared truly on task. Accordingly, this teacher spent more time redirecting behaviors than teaching the content. When the bell rang at the end of the period, the students immediately jumped up from their seats to leave the room. The teacher did not finish his sentence but did appear to be relieved the class was over, as evidenced by the look on his face. I sat there amazed at the difference in the behavior of these students in this class compared to their prior one, and when I met with the principal after school, we discussed my observations.

The principal attributed the problems evident in the last period to poor behavior management skills of the teacher. She was most worried about the disruptions to the learning environment and wanted the teacher to spend much more time dealing with the inappropriate behaviors of the students. Although I agreed behavior concerns were evident, I believed the source of the problem was the learning environment itself. The students were not engaged in the content, which, I believe, led to behavior problems. This was not the case in their previous class where the students were actively involved in the lesson. That teacher focused on providing dynamic instruction, and, as a result, the students' attention was on learning, rather than self-directed activities resulting in misbehavior.

Instruction and Behavior Go Hand in Hand

As discussed in the previous chapter, behavior mainly occurs in a relationship. However, it is not just the teacher-student relationship that determines how behaviors manifest in the classroom. Based on my observations, both teachers in the last example appeared to have good relationships with their students. What resulted in differing student behaviors was the way they taught their classes. If our goal is to prevent misbehavior in the classroom, in addition to building healthy relationships with our students, we must also examine our instructional methods.

Think About It . . .

When you attend professional development, aren't your behaviors mostly determined by the way the presenter (the teacher) runs the session? If you are engaged, you pay attention, contribute, and participate. If not, you might text, scroll through social media, or play a game on your phone. You may even talk to those around you or work on something else. Right? When not engaged in the learning process, adults misbehave in class just as our students do; we just have more practice doing so in a less disruptive way.

Just as there is a relationship between the teacher and student, there is also a relationship between how we teach and student behaviors. So, how do we teach? The short answer is that most teachers' natural inclination is to teach the way we were taught. With most teachers having had at least sixteen years of modeling from our own teachers, we can't help but have internalized methods based on our experiences. This, of course, can create problems because as the world around us changes, so too should our teaching practices.

The Experience of Rituals

Not so long ago, classrooms were filled with students sitting in traditional rows, listening to teachers present lecture-based lessons. In-class assignments and homework were given for comprehension checks, and assessments in the form of either fill-in-the-blanks or essay questions finished out units of study. Classrooms were steeped in consistent rituals which provided a predictable ebb and flow to the school day.

With regard to behavior, there was an unspoken expectation for quiet, passive learning. Most students were compliant and rarely challenged the authority of the teacher. When misbehavior occurred, punishment was the response, which was, for the most part, effective in curtailing or stopping it. However, in today's classroom, these methods don't seem to be as effective as they once were. In order to understand why, we need to look at factors changing outside the school setting that have impacted behaviors within.

Back in the Day

Some of my favorite memories growing up were on long trips taken with my family. We took several trips from Louisiana to Colorado, and in order to get from one location to the next we had to drive through Texas. If you didn't flinch when you read that last sentence, you have never driven from one Texas border to the other. It is a sun-up-to-sun-down experience with very long stretches of never-ending highway. Occasionally signs would indicate we were still in Texas, but they warned us to fill up our gas tanks while we could: next rest stop, 92 miles. Being the last of six children, I was usually crammed in a middle seat, trapped for extended periods with nowhere to go and very little to do. So what held my interest?

- Looking for license plates from different states
- Talking to my siblings . . . or fighting with them
- Listening to Kenny Rogers sing "The Gambler"
- Playing "I Spy"
- Trying to spot the letters of the alphabet on road signs
- Listening to John Denver sing "Grandma's Feather Bed"
- Sitting in silence and just thinking

These experiences taught me how to look for interest in activities that were less than novel. I had to find ways to entertain myself in the absence of a great deal of external stimuli. I also learned how to delay gratification. If I wanted the fun of spending time in Colorado, I had to endure a long car ride and make the best of things. Ultimately, I learned a very important life lesson: you don't always get what you want right when you want it.

Fast-Forward to Today

In today's fast-paced society, instant gratification has become an expectation. Technology has given us the world at our fingertips with one push of a button. We want what we want, and we want it fast. Fast food, fast internet speed, fast networks—all serving to cut down our wait time and provide us with more convenience. But convenience comes at a cost. The more we

In today's fast-paced society, instant gratification has become an expectation.

get what we want right when we want it, the less practice we have being patient and delaying gratification.

We, adults and children alike, have become conditioned to get our needs met quickly, which often translates to less tolerance for lag-time and less acceptance of passivity. If we have to wait too long for any one thing, we are often quick to move on to something else. We bounce around from one thing to the next until our needs are met. The clearest example of this can be found in social media.

Media and Sensationalism

When my wife and I moved to a new city shortly after getting married, I vividly remember turning on the evening news to find the top story. "Are bigger breasts really better? Find out on News at Nine." My jaw hit the ground. Later that same day I picked up the local newspaper and was shocked find *The Star*, a tabloid news feature, as one of the inserts. *This is news?* I thought. Little did I realize at the time that sensationalism would soon become the *norm* of news. And sure enough, as ratings started slipping for news features that were more passive, individuals looked for higher levels of stimulation and novelty became the new focus for garnering TV viewers.

Novelty: The New Norm

Be it video games, TV shows, movies, or the news, stimulation—or, put another way, novelty—has become the new norm. In an attempt to feed the beast of instant gratification, media has become more novel, largely because of our intolerance for less-than-exciting input. We want stimulation that we don't receive when a task, movie, or news feature becomes too repetitive or ritualized. So, we don't sit through whole television shows; we channel surf. Children choose video games with high activity levels—and often sexual, violent, or graphic content—over passive ones. If we take a closer look at the film industry, we find that violence in films has more than doubled since 1950, and gun violence in PG-13-rated films has more than tripled since 1985. When the PG-13 rating was first introduced, these films contained about as much gun violence as G and PG films. Since 2009, PG-13-rated films have contained as much as or more violence than R-rated films.[3] Clearly, we as a culture crave excitement, and that often comes with more violence. And as the world becomes more immersed in a culture of novelty, schools and churches are feeling the impact. The heavy rituals inherent in both the school and church settings do not seem to hold the same level of attention as they once did. In churches, we see the impact of this shift in dramatically lower attendance rates and older congregations. In schools, this change is manifested through students exhibiting more behavior concerns and becoming even more disengaged in learning.

Needed: Self-Regulation Strategies

As the world becomes more externally stimulating, students are in greater need of internal methods to ground and center. Accordingly, it seems more and more schools are teaching the approaches of mindfulness, yoga, breathing techniques, and other self-regulation strategies. The rise in popularity of these approaches, I believe, is a direct result of students being overstimulated with a barrage of novelty outside the walls of the school.

PERSPECTIVE *SHIFT*

"This is boring." It's definitely in the top ten list of phrases I regularly hear from students at school. I also hear it from these children's parents as justification for various problems: "My son misbehaves because he's not challenged. He tells us all the time how boring school is." Having observed students in teachers' classrooms at all levels, I understand the problem. "I'm bored" can mean students are not being challenged, but more often than not, I find it means they are simply not interested in doing the activity presented. I can give a student advanced calculus, which is high rigor, but if he would rather be playing a video game, the problem is not a matter of challenge; it is of interest.

A Balanced Approach

In reality, we need a balance of both ritual and novelty in our lives.

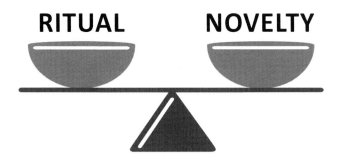

In the classroom, rituals devoid of novelty often lead to boredom and, ultimately, behavior problems.

RITUAL	NOVELTY
Rituals allow our brains to disengage. When we create rituals in the classroom, students can anticipate what's coming next, which lowers anxiety levels and encourages feelings of comfort and safety. Unfortunately, for some students, school is the main source for ritual or schedule in their lives. This could be one reason why weekends, holidays, and summers are difficult for some students. They can't handle the disruption in their routines.	Novelty focuses our attention and increases engagement. When something is new or different, we attend to it. Have you ever tried to hold a conversation with someone who has food in between his teeth? Ketchup on her cheek? As much as you try to block out the visual distraction and listen to the person talking, your brain hyperfocuses and can't attend to anything else. You are held captive by the novelty of the visual distraction.
RITUALS IN EXCESS Although rituals lower anxiety, they also lower our ability to pay attention. When a task becomes too repetitive, rote behaviors kick in and we go into autopilot mode. In the classroom, rituals devoid of novelty often lead to boredom and, ultimately, behavior problems.	**NOVELTY IN EXCESS** Although novelty is exciting, in excess it can heighten anxiety. In the classroom, novelty devoid of classroom rituals can trigger either implosion or explosion, with some students shutting down and others acting out. The classroom with high levels of novelty and few rituals leads to chaos.

Developmental Needs

Teachers who work in the primary grades understand young children need strong classroom rituals. Consistent routines and predictable schedules ground students and help them be able to anticipate the expectations of the teacher. [4] Students also need rituals to balance out the novelty they bring to the classroom. To the young child *everything* is new, so a little bit of novelty goes a long way. When my youngest child Max was in kindergarten, he illustrated this point perfectly. On the last day of school, just before lunch, my son's teacher announced, "Let's all go to the restroom before we leave," at which my son jumped out of his seat and exclaimed, "Yes! I love the bathroom!" He could hardly contain his excitement. The small degree of novelty was all it took to grab his attention and fully engage him.

However, as children get older and move into the higher grade levels, the ritual of school settles in and greater amounts of novelty are needed to positively impact behavior through engagement. As noted, novelty stimulates the brain and focuses attention.[5] Since many older students have internalized the rituals of a class enough to go through the motions of the lessons without really having to engage or attend, they need higher degrees of novelty to effectively balance out the scales. Each grade level and group of students is unique, but the key is to find the balance that works.

Strategies for Embedding Rituals and Novelty

Teachers need to develop strong rituals in the classroom, but we also need to infuse novelty into our instructional practices. By providing both, we increase the likelihood students will engage in learning and decrease their opportunities for misbehavior. Listed below are specific strategies for employing both.

Rituals

Keep a Consistent Schedule

When schedules are consistently followed, students are able to anticipate expectations and plan accordingly. Schedules also allow students time to predict and adjust to changes from one event to the next. Post the daily agenda for ease of reference. Some students benefit from having a visual schedule that can be followed using a clothespin or other marker. This visual and tactile strategy helps make the schedule more concrete.

Shorten Transitions

Avoid lags during transition times. Transitions often introduce the novelty of having less structure. This can invite problems since novelty can serve to escalate inappropriate behaviors. Avoid this problem by having clear procedures in place for transitions. Continually practice the transitions to the point of habituation.

Provide Strong Beginnings and Endings

Have clear openings and closings to lessons, articulating time frames for activities. When students have a clear understanding of when activities start and stop, the brain can better anticipate expectations and prepare accordingly. Consider using a countdown timer students can follow to know when lessons and activities start and end.

Integrate "Belonging" Rituals

When students are consistently greeted at the door, have class handshakes, or repeat chants or callbacks known by the whole class, they feel a sense of belonging. These rituals not only help the students better connect with the class community but also foster a sense of common understanding of the shared practice.

Prepare Students for Change

As the adage goes, "The only thing constant is change." Help students prepare for the invariable disruptions to the routines that will take place throughout the school day by using words of caution: "We might have to flip this activity depending on when the speaker arrives," or "Remember, we are having a fire drill sometime today. Let's review the procedures we need to follow."

Provide Students with Jobs

Give students regular roles and responsibilities to carry out throughout the school day so they are more likely to internalize class rituals. When student jobs are integrated into daily activities, such as passing out papers and taking books to the media center, students are also more likely to keep rituals in place in the teacher's absence. This practice not only strengthens classroom rituals, but also encourages students to self-regulate their routines.

Avoid the "Countdown": "We only have five more days until we get out for break, so I need you to stay with me. We have a lot of content  to cover." Often teachers inadvertently create anxiety in students by continually referring to the novelty of upcoming changes in the schedule. This escalates negative behavior in some students. It's okay to prepare students for upcoming changes, but doing so repeatedly can inadvertently raise anxiety in them.

Novelty

Teach in Different Locations

When we teach from the same location in the room each day, we become a "fixture." Have you ever seen the glazed-over look from your students or feel as though they are not paying attention even when they are looking straight at you? This can happen more readily when we stay in the same location each day. Seeing the same visual background repeatedly causes their brains to lose focus and inadvertently wander off. Avoid this potential lag in attention by regularly teaching content in different areas of the room. The simple change in background can provide just enough novelty to keep students focused for longer periods of time.

Vary Your Voice Tone, Volume, and Rate of Speech

Just as students can lose visual interest in the class, so, too, can they tune out voices that are heard over and over again. When we vary the tone, volume, and rate of our speech while teaching, interest and attention levels rise. Teachers who talk a great deal in class see the impact of this strategy simply by remaining quiet for about fifteen seconds during a lesson. The second the teacher stops talking, students attend. The novelty of the silence refocuses all students in the room. After trying this strategy for the first time with one of my classes, I had a student approach me. "Mr. St. Romain, when you stopped talking, we were worried. We thought you had died or something—because that never happens."

Integrate Novelty into Review Activities

Class reviews are a perfect time to integrate novelty into the lessons. Use game formats like Password, 20 Questions, Jeopardy, and Bingo to solidify content and check for understanding with your students. I often taught new content Monday through Thursday and used Fridays to review content. Not only did my absences on Friday drop dramatically, but behavior problems seemed less apparent on these days, and attention and interest levels rose in the process—simply because I was infusing more novelty and reviewing content in a way that was engaging for the students.

Use Music and Chants

Older teachers who are familiar with *School House Rock* understand the power of this strategy. "Conjunction Junction, what's your function?" When content is put in a format that integrates music, chants, or gestures, students are more likely to be involved in the learning and less likely to engage in misbehavior. The novelty of the format not only helps with engagement, but strengthens retention of the content as well.

Use Props and Visuals

Interesting visual aids and tangible props go a long way in not only holding student attention but helping students remember content as well. The more unusual the image or prop, the higher the novelty factor will be.

Let Students Teach Students

Encouraging students to share information with each other is a powerful way to capitalize on the use of novelty in the classroom. This can be done in pairs or small and large group settings. The key is having the students hear the content from someone other than the same person who usually teaches the content.

Break Up Content into Smaller Chunks

We remember content better when information is broken up into smaller chunks. We also "reset" our attention clock when we start something new. For example, in a ninety-minute block, consider teaching two forty-minute lessons broken up with a ten-minute novel review activity in between.

Vary Assessment Techniques

Provide different measures for assessing growth and progress. Project-based assessments, group reports and presentations, journal entries, and infomercials will raise interest levels. These methods do not have to be the final assessments (which might need to be conducted using traditional paper-and-pencil methods), but they can help focus attention and provide comprehension checks along the way.

Engagement is not entertainment.

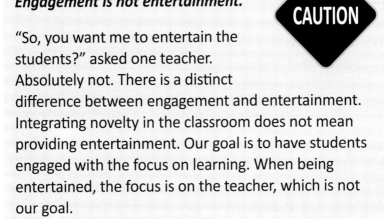

"So, you want me to entertain the students?" asked one teacher. Absolutely not. There is a distinct difference between engagement and entertainment. Integrating novelty in the classroom does not mean providing entertainment. Our goal is to have students engaged with the focus on learning. When being entertained, the focus is on the teacher, which is not our goal.

Infusing novelty is also not about being a certain personality type. Not everyone is high energy, type A, and outgoing, though these are the teachers who often get all the attention. Not all students relate to this type of teacher. The goal is not to be a certain type of teacher; the goal is for teachers to infuse novelty in a way that works for them. This will look different in every classroom, based on the age of the students, as well as the style of the teacher.

Novelty usually escalates behaviors at first.

When new activities are introduced in the classroom, it is very common for students to talk a bit more, get a little silly, and need more frequent redirection. This should be expected. Avoid the trap of telling students, "I see, you can't handle this," and abandoning the activity. Instead, work through the novelty and teach the students how to do so. As the newness wears off, behaviors will improve. The goal is to find the balance.

In Summary . . .

Rituals provide structure, consistency, and feelings of safety. This is best accomplished when students are afforded predictable routines and consistently followed procedures and rules. Although rituals are critical in the classroom, they must be balanced with novelty. Novelty both focuses students' attention and keeps them engaged in learning.

When teachers have strong rituals with too little novelty, students may become disengaged, at which time behavior problems can arise. The more ritualized the classroom, the less novelty it takes for students to be distracted with attention drawn away from learning. When there is an absence of novelty, students meet this need by talking or moving, both of which can be disruptive to the learning process. However, when teachers infuse a great deal of novelty without strong rituals in place, anxiety often increases and behaviors escalate. Effective teaching requires a balance of the two: rituals for order and consistency, and novelty for interest and engagement.

FINAL THOUGHT

By creating a healthy balance of rituals and novelty in the classroom, attention to task increases and behavioral concerns decrease.

PREVENTION
80%

PRINCIPLE
THREE

It Is Easier to Channel Behavior Than to Stop It

Just a Few More Slides to Go

I have a reputation, and it's not one that I want. It seems I'm not always the best workshop participant, which is ironic since I have a never-ending thirst for learning. This is an especially embarrassing thing to admit since the majority of my career has been spent providing staff development. Unfortunately, my style of learning can be at odds with the teaching style of some teachers. I came to this realization early in my career when I attended a full-day staff development session on differentiated instruction. At the time, this was a new initiative and focus for many schools. Being relatively new to the profession, I was looking forward to seeing how I could use this information to strengthen my teaching skills.

As I recall, there were about six of us from my school sitting at our table, including my supervisor, our principal. Prior to the start of the workshop, she let us know it would be our job to each take a portion of the content learned and present it to the faculty when we returned to our school. I was already interested in the information, but this new level of accountability increased my motivation and need to pay attention.

I was relieved when the workshop materials were handed out, as the bound manual was about an inch thick. I knew at that point, I had a good resource I could use when presenting the information to our faculty. However, I remember being surprised at the layout of the information. Each page of the entire manual detailed six PowerPoint slides with the content noted in exponentially small print. I was overwhelmed, to say the least.

After introducing herself (slide #1), the presenter outlined the schedule (slide #2) and objectives (slide #3) for our day, and then dove into the content. It was great information and my brain was whirling, but I had questions and, to my principal's great annoyance, many other thoughts and comments. "How can I adapt this in a small group setting?" "This would be a great assessment." "What section do I want to present to the faculty?" I continually turned to my neighbors with editorial comments, accompanied by many nasty glances from my principal.

I made it to the first break without major incident, but I remember distinctly, when we settled back in afterward, being frustrated at the fast pace at which we were moving through the content. I had little to no time in between sections to talk and process the information. As the morning continued, a second problem surfaced—I started to twitch. As a classroom teacher, I was used to moving around the room continuously. My body was not accustomed to sitting stagnantly for long periods of time. Of course, the principal was the first to notice the entire table shaking, courtesy of my leg which was bouncing up and down underneath it.

My last memory of this day was just after lunch. By this point, I had shut down. I couldn't take in any more information, so I spent the time calculating. "Let's see. We have fifty-two more pages to go, with six slides per page. That's 312 more slides, divided by two and a half hours, minus the fifteen-minute break . . ." When my neighbor discovered what I was doing, laughter ensued, which led to disruptive behaviors for the remainder of the afternoon.

I felt bad. I knew my behavior detracted attention from the content, which was not my plan. I *wanted* to learn about the content, but my brain needed to be given opportunities to actively process the information through purposeful discussion and movement. Learners need to talk and move, and if their brains are not given opportunities to do both, behavior problems are likely to surface.

Brain Channels

We learned about the five basic senses of sound, sight, smell, touch, and taste early in our education. Each of these senses serves as a road, passageway, or channel through which information from the outside world enters our brains. This information is the foundation of learning modalities, or the way in which students learn using their senses. Although there are five senses, most theorists identify the three broad categories of visual, auditory, and kinesthetic as the main avenues through which we learn new information.[6] Visual information is taken in through sight. Auditory information is taken in through sound. Kinesthetic information is taken in through touch.

MODALITIES

AUDITORY

VISUAL   KINESTHETIC

When information on modalities (or learning styles, as referenced by some) was first introduced, there was a strong push to assess and categorize students' preferences for learning accordingly—the idea being that if we know how a student prefers to learn, it would be beneficial to teach the child using that same modality. Although individuals do have preferences for learning, there is no evidence that teaching them in that specific mode yields better outcomes. Additionally, by categorizing students as being visual, auditory, or kinesthetic, we run the risk of boxing them in based on their preferences. In reality, we use all three modalities for learning. It is for this reason theorists recommend taking a much broader approach to how we use information on learning modalities in teaching.

Auditory Traffic Jam

Traditional models of teaching rely heavily on lecture-based, direct-teach instruction. This method puts a lot of strain on the auditory cortex, the structure in the brain processing our modality of sound. This can create a backup of information going into the brain, similar to what occurs in a traffic jam. When too many vehicles are trying to enter the same highway, traffic comes to a halt. This is how lecture-based instruction often plays out. When we only input information through the channel of sound, auditory overload occurs, causing students to tune out teachers and misbehave. The brain can only take in so much information before it shuts down. Gary Larson in his *Far Side* cartoon captured this idea beautifully. A student raises his hand in the classroom and says to his teacher, "Mr. Osborne, may I be excused? My brain is full." This is a common phenomenon in the classroom—content overload. And when the brain is full, the brain shuts down.

Have you ever gotten caught in a traffic jam? If you are like most individuals, your first line of defense is to look for an alternate route to get you where you are going. You take a feeder or frontage road and get out of the congestion as quickly as possible—the situation triggering stress in you. This is similar to what happens with some students in the classroom setting. They get overloaded with auditory information, which causes stress, in turn triggering misbehavior. However, we can proactively head off the traffic jam of misbehavior by identifying the needs and concerns before they arise and meeting the needs accordingly.

Multi-Modal Teaching: Change the Channel

As discussed in the last chapter, effective teaching incorporates a balance of ritual and novelty. When we become too heavy-handed with the ritual of lecture-based instruction, the infusion of novelty can help focus attention and have a positive impact on student behaviors. One of the best ways to infuse novelty is to mix up the way we teach, allowing visual and kinesthetic channels to be opened up and used in addition to auditory ones. Finding ways to use multiple methods for getting information into the brain not only alleviates brain congestion but also helps students better retain the concepts presented. This type of teaching is referred to as multimodal instruction, and although there are cognitive benefits to utilizing these strategies, these methods can also have a positive impact on student behavior.

Think About It . . .

When learning, what is your preference? Listening? Watching? Doing? Over the years I have posed this question continuously to large groups of teachers. Without fail, the majority of participants prefer to learn by watching and, without fail, the fewest prefer to learn by listening (with "doers" somewhere in the middle). This seems ironic, given that the primary way we teach students, pre-kindergarten through high school, is through auditory instruction.

"Stop That"

Have you ever heard of Restless Leg Syndrome (RLS)? The struggle is real. A tingling sensation creeps throughout your leg, and the longer you sit still, the worse the sensation gets. When you finally relent and move your leg, the tingling stops . . . for about a minute, at which time the cycle repeats. And to make matters worse, RLS usually overtakes a person at the worst possible times—when trapped on an airplane or trying to sleep. And, unfortunately, ignoring the problem only makes things

> *When a person has a need that is not getting met, the brain finds a way to get the need met.*

worse. RLS often triggers frustration and anger, which is understandable. When a person has a need that is not getting met, the brain finds a way to get the need met.

We all know students who need to talk and move. I call these two methods *instructional* basic needs. Teachers can try to suppress these needs, but as is the case with RLS, the brain finds a way to get the needs met. For me, it was by talking. I was an incessant talker in school. My brain was constantly processing information, and in order for it to make sense, I needed to talk. This was a problem, as my teachers had a goal—to get me (and others like me) to stop talking. I had other friends who had a different need—to move. Sitting still for long periods of time was a challenge for them. Their brains were telling them to move, but, again, the teacher's goal was to stop the movement.

Feed the Needs: Talking and Moving

 **PERSPECTIVE SHIFT**

As a consultant, I'm often confronted by teachers wanting me to help them find ways to get their students to stop talking and be quiet. Upon reflection, I question the end

result of this goal. Do we really want quiet learners? Anyone who works with teenagers knows the importance of teaching social register and appropriate expression of thoughts. And anyone who works with young children knows language development is a critical educational goal. So, do we really want quiet learners? Or do we want learners who are given time to talk while also learning the social convention of listening and not interrupting when appropriate?

When I ask teachers about behavior problems the issues of excessive talking and movement always surface. "How can I get them to stop?" I'm asked. My response to this question is consistent. "My recommendation is that we don't focus on stopping these behaviors. Quite the opposite." I liken the instructional needs of talking and moving to a body of water. If a flood is coming our way, it is very challenging to stop it. The better approach is to *channel* it. Encouraging students to talk and move through instruction allows them to get these needs met in a positive way, lessening the chance these needs will get met in a way that disrupts the learning in the classroom.

Geoffrey and Renate Caine identified two learning principles on the need for movement and social interaction close to three decades ago in the book *Making Connections: Teaching and the Human Brain.*[7] Although their body of work surrounding the brain-based principles has expanded, the core tenets of two of them support this idea of channeling behavior:

The Brain/Mind Is Social

As humans, we are social beings. We have an innate need to connect and belong. Affording students time to talk, reflect, and interact with peers in the classroom benefits teaching and learning in several ways:

Social Interaction/Talking

- Is a life skill
- Helps meet the need for a sense of belonging
- Relieves stress
- Affords students time to process information
- Improves the overall class climate
- Helps students process the information differently
- Increases retention of information
- Allows students time to talk (a very high need for some)

"I don't need time to talk," a student once told me. "I'm an introvert and like to work alone." Through follow-up discussions and reflection time, the student had two realizations:

1. Although his preference was to work alone, it was good for him to practice the life skill of working with others.
2. He discovered he did need talk time, just internally. "I do talk. I just talk things over in my own head—to myself. Does that sound weird?"

Learning Engages the Entire Physiology

Teaching and learning are not stagnant processes. The brain and body work together. Our ability to take in information is impacted by our physical state. If our physical needs are not met, learning will be inhibited.

Physical Activity/Movement

- Increases oxygen to the brain
- Increases neuronal activity
- Increases blood flow
- Focuses attention
- Speeds up processing of information
- Increases retention of information
- Relieves stress
- Allows students time to move (a very high need for some)

Strategies for Channeling Behavior

There are many easy strategies that can be implemented into teachers daily teaching strategies which allow behaviors to be channeled. The key is to turn these strategies into predictable rituals and habits so students' needs for talk time and movement are met proactively. Listed below are some simple suggestions for both.

Socialization

Have Students Work in Groups

Small and large group social interaction affords students an opportunity to be part of a team, while also giving them practice using social skills with diverse people in diverse settings. This is a critical skill they will use in life, long after they transition from the school setting.

Utilize "Turn and Talks"

Break up teaching sections by having students turn and talk to a neighbor about the content. This can be a very effective way to not only provide students an opportunity to talk, but also review content, check for understanding, and help refocus attention on the topic at hand.

Get into the Teaching Habit of Using Callbacks During Instruction

Reinforce concepts by having the students call back key pieces of information. When giving directions or teaching content, have students repeat words or phrases as a check for understanding, as well as for retention of information.

Note: When callbacks are first introduced, students might be hesitant to repeat information. This is normal and expected, as the novelty of doing so can be embarrassing. However, once callbacks are part of the culture and rituals of the class, students will participate accordingly.

Have Students Talk with One Partner

When discussions arise as part of a class group, usually the same students volunteer information and the majority of students remain quiet. When students work with one partner:

- They are afforded more talk time.
- They are more likely to share information when talking with a friend.
- They are held to a higher standard of accountability for talking and interacting.

Use Closed-Ended Questions

Build the expectation for choral responses using questions that force specific responses. "Make sense? Yes or no?" If the large majority of students don't respond, repeat the question. "Couldn't hear that. Yes or no?" As the expectation of an answer is practiced, the response will become a class ritual.

Note: Not all students will participate in the call and response. As long as the majority do so, the ritual will become a habit. Remember, the main idea is to allow students the opportunity to speak, decreasing the likelihood they might do so in a way that often disrupts learning.

Be careful not to inadvertently condition your students to be silent. I hear this from teachers regularly: "When I ask my students a question, the response is usually one of complete silence," or "I posed a question to my students and no one wants to volunteer information." I believe this problem to be one of conditioning. When we create the expectation for our learners to listen while we talk, we have to be careful not to ingrain the behavior to the point where they are hesitant to volunteer the information. Put another way, when our learners get into a *ritual* of listening for an extended period of time, they will be less likely to respond when posed with the *novelty* of being asked a question. We can combat this problem by infusing more interactive discussions when teaching.

Movement

Assign Areas for Learning

Provide different areas of the classroom for students to work: reading nooks, project tables, small group discussion areas. Have students move to the other side of the room or to one of the four corners during assigned times. Another option is to have the students move from one desk pod to another desk pod for different activities. Each group can have a different task or topic on which to work.

Use Gestures to Reinforce Content

Encourage students to use gestures visually and kinesthetically representing concepts learned. To this day, I unconsciously cross my arms when I think of the word perpendicular and put my arms straight out when I hear the words parallel. These were gestures I learned decades ago—and I still remember them.

Initially, teachers need to model examples of making up gestures to represent concepts. However, once students get comfortable with the idea, they can work in groups or individually to do so. This activity helps the students channel their need for movement while also teaching them a powerful strategy for retaining content through kinesthetic cues.

Have Students Swap Chairs and Sit in a Different Area of the Classroom

Sitting in a different area of the room meets the need for movement, and it also provides a degree of novelty that can help with both attention and retention of content. When sitting at tables, have the students stand up to find a partner and report to any new table in the room. This is also a great strategy for interrupting discussions between two students without singling them out. If two students are having a side conversation during instruction, teachers can instruct the whole class to switch chairs and find new seat partners.

Review Content in Different Locations of the Classroom

Place posters of content at different desks or on different walls around the room. Encourage students to move around and visit each of the stations, reviewing the concepts. Music can be used to signal students to move from location to location.

Go for Learning Walks or Move the Class to a New Location

At times, the energy level of the class can drop dramatically. Since learning engages the entire physiology, have the students find a partner and go for a walk while reviewing concepts. The entire class can walk together around the track or to a new location in the building for instruction.

Prompt Students to Provide Feedback Physically

Have students respond using visual cues throughout the day.

- "Raise your hand if that makes sense."
- "Point to the poster that best illustrates that concept."
- "Thumbs up or thumbs down?"
- "Show me. Really high or really low?"

Each of these prompts encourages students to physically move to provide the response. These responses also give the teacher feedback on concepts learned.

The extension activity below is another great way for students to provide instructional feedback physically.

ACTIVITY

Place a rating scale of numbers 1–10 around the room. Teach the students the rating.

1   2   3   4   5   6   7   8   9   10

- **1** – *I'm completely lost and can't even begin to understand this concept.*
- **4** – *I sort of understand but still have a lot of questions.*
- **7** – *I understand this concept.*
- **10** – *I could easily teach this concept.*

After teaching a new concept, prompt students to use the rating scale. "We just learned about how democracy works. Stand by the number that best represents your understanding of this information." This activity provides the teacher with great feedback on the effectiveness of lessons. Afterward, partner up "6–10" students with "1–5" students for a reteach and practice. This puts some students in leadership roles, allowing concepts to be reinforced in varied ways.

Use Toss Objects

Use toss objects and fidget toys to encourage simple motor movements. Whoever has the object is the person who talks. This activity can be used in small groups or in a whole class setting. Objects can range from small bean bags to stuffed animals to large beach balls. Referring to the last principle of novelty and ritual, younger students usually need less novel an activity to channel the need for movement (quietly passing a ball from person to person), whereas older students will probably need an activity that has higher impact (for example, tossing an object around a group until the music stops).

Assign Jobs Encouraging Movement

Teachers work too hard. Alleviate this problem by having students pass out materials, go on errands, rearrange desks, take attendance, etc. These are especially important jobs for students who have a stronger need for movement than others.

Teach Students About the Importance of Movement

Inherently, when we are given reasons and have an understanding for why we are being asked to do something, we are more likely to comply. Help students understand the critical role movement plays in learning. Pre-teach the different strategies you will use throughout the school year to meet the need for movement and encourage students to get their needs met accordingly.

There are two "I'd, buts" I hear regularly when recommending that teachers embed more movement and talk time into their lessons:

1. *"I'd* let my students talk about the lessons we are learning, *but* they never talk about what they are supposed to be talking about. They just misbehave."

   Healthy relationships are based in trust, so when students are talking with each other, **assume positive intent**. I know students might talk about other things when I give them prompts to discuss. I *assume* their conversation is important and trust they will also follow my directions. The reason I give my students time to talk is to provide them opportunities to get their thoughts out under my direction, as I know this will decrease the amount of time they will talk about other things while I am teaching. One way to have some accountability is to assign a reporter to each group when you have them discuss a learning point. The reporter's job is to report back a summary of the group's discussions to the class.

2. *"I'd* integrate more movement and activities into my lessons, *but* the students can't handle it. They go crazy."

   When you introduce a new activity to your students involving movement, you are introducing novelty, which always escalates behavior at first. As noted in the last chapter, rather than depriving them of the opportunity to move, *teach* them how to handle the activity, knowing the more you practice and the more the novelty wears off, the better students will get at carrying it out.

In Summary . . .

Too often, adults try to stop students from exhibiting two instructional basic needs: talking and moving. Although these behaviors can be disruptive in the classroom, it is important to understand they serve important functions. When students talk or move during instruction, they are providing feedback about their needs to the teacher. Rather than trying to stop these behaviors, a more effective approach is to channel them. By using chants, songs, activities, and other multi-modal means to teach, students are given healthy outlets for getting their needs met appropriately. This is especially important for young children who may not have the capacity to stay still or remain quiet for long periods of time.

FINAL THOUGHT

The more purposefully we embed opportunities for discussion and movement into our instruction, the less likely students will be to meet these needs on their own in a way that disrupts learning.

Modeled Behaviors Are Internalized

One of my favorite articles was written by a graduate professor of mine, Dr. James Garbarino. Though I came across it early in my career, it made quite an impact on me, and I think about it often. "Our Response to the Attack on America: What Can It Teach Children About Understanding and Revenge?" was written following the terrorist attacks on September 11, 2001.[8] In it, Dr. Garbarino validated my own feelings of frustration and anger following the tragedy, but he helped individuals look beyond the event itself at how our responses to it will impact children. The gist of the article emphasized that 911 presented adults with an opportunity to teach a variety of lessons to children: fear, revenge, empathy, hatred, understanding, prejudice, compassion. However, the lessons kids learned would depend on what the adults around them chose to say and do in response. I believe this to always be the case, and it is something educators need to remember. As the article simply put it: "Our kids are watching and listening."

Do As I Say, Not As I Do

Anthony was an articulate young man. Truth be told, I believe there was a forty-year-old philosopher trapped inside his sixteen-year-old body. He had been placed in a residential treatment center long before I worked there. And because he both lived and went to school there, he had seen and heard a lot from both students and staff. He was anything but shy, which meant he rarely held back his thoughts. Most often I would hear about his concerns when he was brought to me for some cool-off time after having a behavioral meltdown. He regularly got on soapboxes, expounding about all that was good and bad in the world, and, one day in particular, he gave me an earful.

"Hypocrisy, I tell you! That's what I call it. You can't fool me. My teacher tells me I'm in here because of my attitude. What about her attitude? I was trying to find my journal, but I couldn't. I can't help it if I've got a lot of stuff in my backpack! Mrs. Simone said, 'It's alright, Anthony. Take your time. We're not waiting on you.' All the kids in the class started laughing, but I didn't think it was funny. So, I said, 'Good, then I'll take my time.' She didn't like that at all. She said, 'Don't take that tone with me, Anthony,' and when I said, 'You started it!' she sent me out of the room. How come she can talk to me like that, but I can't do the same to her? Mr. Phillip is the same way. He tells me to keep my voice down all the time—that I'm too loud. But he screams at all of us when he gets mad. How's that right?"

I started to ask Anthony a question but didn't have the opportunity. He continued. "Mrs. Cyndy never does that. She's always nice, even when she's having a bad day. That teacher knows how to treat people. She could show Ms. Simone and Mr. Phillip a thing or two about that."

To this day I can still hear Anthony preaching about the injustices of the world. Though at times sensationalized, many of his points were valid. If we want students to learn appropriate behaviors, we must be certain our words and actions align in a positive way.

Learned Behaviors

As discussed in the last chapter, information is taken in through the brain using our visual, auditory, and kinesthetic senses. These three modalities lay the foundation for learning. If our goal is to help children in the school setting learn appropriate behaviors, it is important to understand the two ways this can happen: through direct instruction and modeling.

1. Direct Instruction

Schools use direct instruction as the main method for teaching. Targeted skills are broken down into distinct steps and then taught accordingly. Teachers introduce concepts through initial instruction, provide time for practice, and assess competency. If warranted, the three-step process is repeated until skills are mastered. Direct instruction is an experience that shapes our behaviors on a conscious level, meaning the learner is aware of and attending to the process. This is most often not the case when we learn through modeling.

2. Modeling

Throughout our development, the sights and sounds we experience on a daily basis play a large part in shaping our behaviors. The brain is wired for survival, so it internalizes input from the outside world and learns and adapts however needed to accomplish this task. Thus, we learn by watching and interacting with others. Most of what we take in through the modeling of others happens on an unconscious level.

In looking back at Anthony's experience, his perception was that what Mrs. Simone and Mr. Phillip did was not modeling the respectful behaviors they expected him to use through direct instruction. He did, however, note how positively Mrs. Cyndy treated him. The more we are able to model the behaviors we are teaching, the more likely we are to send consistent messages, thus increasing the chance for students to internalize the concepts.

Many learned behaviors are the result of both direct instruction and modeling. Language development is a great example of this. Students might be introduced to a new word through a vocabulary unit (direct instruction), but their understanding of the word is deepened when they hear it used by others in context (modeling). The more the word is heard, the more information is added to their bank of understanding. At some point, the word spills over into vocabulary, influencing language aspects of their behavior.

Actions Speak Louder than Words

When my boys were young, I was insistent on teaching them manners. I had a whole bank of words and phrases I was determined to incorporate into their daily vocabulary. Without exception, I expected them to say "Please," "Thank you," "You're welcome," "Excuse me," and because I'm a good Southern boy, "Yes/No Ma'am" and "Yes/No Sir." It was at the dinner table where my children received my direct instruction learning and practicing this skill. If they wanted to eat, they needed to use their manners. "Can I have some milk?" my oldest would ask. "Try again," was my reply. "May I *please* have some milk?" he would say. "Of course," was my response. And without fail, after receiving the milk I would stare at him patiently until he nicely uttered the words, "Thank you," to me. The work paid off because after some time all four of my children got very good at using these manner words at the dinner table.

Unfortunately, my oldest son taught me the first error of my ways one night when we sat down at the dinner table. I looked across the table and uttered a phrase I used regularly to my wife, "That looks good. Pass me that dish." After my wife passed it to me, my eldest looked at me with his big blue eyes and inquired, "How come you didn't say 'please' . . . or 'thank you' . . . or 'you're welcome'?" It was a valid question, and one for which I really didn't have an answer. Telling him that my wife and I had moved beyond the *novelty* stage of marriage and settled into the *ritual* phase where manners are no longer a central focus would have just confused him. My sons were receiving mixed messages. I taught my boys to use manners, but I wasn't always modeling my expectations in my day-to-day living. So much for the power of direct instruction.

The second problem I discovered was one of location and generalization. When we were at the dinner table, I focused on teaching manners. It seemed like a logical time to do so. After all, we ate every night, we were all around the dinner table, and my children were hungry, so I had a captive audience. However, when we ventured out in public, I wasn't as consistent about my expectations, so I didn't see those manner-based expectations transfer as readily into everyday settings. They demonstrated manners in the context I taught them but failed to generalize those same behaviors elsewhere.

When it comes to behavior, both direct teaching and modeling have their place, but as illustrated in my story above, if students aren't afforded the opportunity to learn and practice behaviors in a variety of settings, or if adults consistently model behaviors contrary to what is being taught, our teaching efforts will not yield positive results.

> *Because our habits are so repetitive, our children have more opportunities to learn behaviors through our modeling than through our direct instruction.*

One of the benefits and dangers of modeling is that it is usually the gift that keeps on giving. When teaching in isolation, we are aware and conscious of our instruction. We are strategic and purposeful about what we say and do. However, because most modeling is the result of habits we have developed, it is usually unconscious. If we have gotten into good habits, we will teach positive behaviors. Unfortunately, the opposite is also true. Our own poor habits will transfer through modeling as well. Because our habits are so repetitive, our children have more opportunities to learn behaviors through our modeling than through our direct instruction.

Additionally, modeling usually occurs in context, which is more natural and fluent and provides more meaning. All of these factors increase the likelihood children internalize modeled behaviors, more so, I believe, than through direct instruction.

Societal Modeling and Mixed Messages

The beauty of living in a free society is . . . freedom. In America, individuals have freedom of speech and can express themselves openly. This can be a good thing; however, our choices have a direct impact on our consequences. I believe many concerning behaviors our youth exhibit are a direct result of the modeling they receive from adults in our society. If we don't like the resulting behaviors of our youth, we need to question whether as a society we are sending consistent or mixed messages when it comes to our words and actions. I believe it to be the latter. This is most especially the case with regard to pop culture and the role of technology in teaching.

When one of my sons was very young, I walked by as he was watching a very aggressive fight scene on television, which ended with the stabbing and subsequent death of one of the characters. When my son saw the concerned look on my face he said, "Daddy, it's okay. He was the *bad* guy." I remember asking him, "So, do you think it's okay to hurt someone if you are the *good* guy?" After immediately responding with a yes, he stopped, scratched his head, and looked at me with a confused expression on his face. I remember walking away just as confused.

I'm not implying that violence is never justified, but at that moment I realized the mixed messages my son was receiving. We tell him to use his words to solve his problems rather than hitting, yet action movies, reality TV, and talk shows often glamorize physical aggression as a common and expected practice. My son's reasoning troubled me as well—it's okay to hurt someone if you are the good guy. The problem with this perspective is that we all think we are the good guys. My students in behavior units often justified their actions by claiming the *good guy* position: "Don't get mad at me. I'm the good guy. Yes. I hit him, but he deserved it. If he didn't want that to happen, he shouldn't have looked at me that way." If I'm teaching my child to use his words to solve problems, it is important for him to see adults model this same behavior.

The Parenting Challenge

I'm often told, "Wow. You must be a really good father since you are a behavior consultant." I usually answer, "No. I'm a great father . . . for other people's children." If you are an educator and parent, you understand the struggle. I might know exactly how I'm supposed to respond as a teacher when my students exhibit inappropriate behaviors, but when my own children do the same, all my knowledge, skills, and strategies get thrown out of the window. I might never raise my voice with a student, but I can't say I'm able to do the same with my own children. I totally understand why modeling is more difficult for parents.

Parents' strong emotional connections to their children make it difficult to approach behavioral challenges with objectivity. Thus, children's inappropriate behaviors often bring out the same in their parents. Additionally, parents are with their children for far longer periods of time than teachers. Even when I wake up in a bad mood, as a teacher I can put on my game face and model appropriate behaviors for a limited amount of time during the school day. However, as a parent I'm always "on," which makes it harder to continuously model appropriate behaviors. My own children see the good, the bad, and the ugly. Since children don't always see the best of their parents' behaviors, appropriate modeling from teachers becomes even more important.

Nonparent Caring Adults

Students benefit from healthy adult role models aside from their parents. This idea is highlighted in research from Search Institute.[9] The Developmental Assets is a framework identifying forty positive supports youth need for successful development. The first strand identifies the importance of support: "Young people need to be surrounded by people who love, care for, appreciate, and accept them." Within this strand, the specific asset of "other adult relationships" is identified: "Young people receive support from three or more nonparent adults."[10] Aside from parents, teachers are the adults with whom most children spend the majority of their time, so their impact as important role models is critical.

Modeling Strategies

When outlining strategies for modeling appropriate behaviors, there are four important factors teachers need to examine. The better we are able to teach through our modeling in these areas, the better the chance we have to positively impact student behaviors.

1. Body Language

One of my students taught me about the importance of body language. Larry regularly complained to me about one thing or another, but when he got really frustrated, he would fall into the same mantra: "Stop yelling at me!" he would say. This confused me, as I have many faults, but yelling at students was not one of them. Though I often got frustrated, I was able to keep the volume and tone of my voice under control. My response to him was consistent, "I'm not yelling, Larry." This comment didn't help the situation.

It was my instructional assistant, Irma, who helped me understand the problem. "I can't understand why he says I'm yelling. I don't raise my voice," I told her. She just smiled. "Every time you approach him with your arms crossed, he says, 'you are yelling.' It's your body language, not your volume." I had never really considered that. As I recall, I crossed my arms often because our classroom was always freezing, though my reasoning didn't matter. Larry's perception of my body language triggered his defensiveness. I was modeling the very behaviors that triggered his behavior. From that time forward, I made a concerted effort not to cross my arms when redirecting him, and, sure enough, he stopped calling me out for yelling.

Crossed arms, hands on the hips, and facial expressions are all aspects of body language we need to take into consideration when working with students. Our goal is to make certain our body language conveys the same positive message as our words and actions.

2. Words

Choose words carefully. The words we use and the way we phrase things on a daily basis shape both the vocabulary and language habits of our students. I teach students that our brains can act as a filter. If we think about the words that come out of our mouths before we say them, our brains can help us keep the negative thoughts out and let the positive comments pass. As we've all learned, "If we don't have something nice to say, we probably shouldn't say anything at all."

THINK before you speak.

Is it **T**rue?

Is it **H**elpful?

Is it **I**nspiring?

Is it **N**ecessary?

Is it **K**ind?

If we want students to *think* before they speak, adults need to model this behavior.

3. Voice Volume

Our goal is for the volume of our voice to match the appropriateness of the setting. Walk through the halls of a school building and listen to teachers and you will quickly discover that this is an easier task for some than others.

A loud volume in and of itself might not be a concern; however, when coupled with negative tone, words, or body language, the result works against our efforts to elicit positive behaviors in our students. A loud voice is also more likely to elicit the same from a student, which is not a reaction we want to encourage.

4. Tone

Our tone is reflected by our voice inflection. Tone comes across not necessarily in *what* we say but, rather, in *how* we say it. When teaching this concept to students, I refer to tone as one's vocal attitude. Our tone can convey frustration, disgust, and superiority. It can also express encouragement, understanding, and concern. The goal for adults, of course, is the latter.

Think About It . . .

In the past few decades, the use of sarcasm seems to have grown and become commonplace in our everyday language. One way to define sarcasm is a type of humor directed at the expense of self or others (usually others). Literally, the origin of the word can be traced to the Greek word sarkazein, meaning to tear flesh or to speak bitterly. Either way it is defined, the use of sarcasm is not usually thought of in a positive way. When students use sarcasm with peers, it seems hurtful. When students use sarcasm with adults, it seems disrespectful. So, the best rule is to avoid its use altogether.

PERSPECTIVE *SHIFT*

At times, teachers get into the habit of using sarcasm with students through questioning:

- *"Do you want me to buzz the office?"*

- *"Do you like it when I call your mother?"*

- *"Do you want me to sign your folder?"*

If an administrator were to do the same to teachers, I wonder how the information would be received:

- *"Do you want to get paid?"*

- *"Do you like having to write your lesson plans over the weekend?"*

Note: *Awareness of modeling is critical in times of stress. When we are calm, and stress levels are low, we often model positive behaviors. However, when in highly stressful situations, we are most at risk for modeling the very behaviors we wish to extinguish in our students. It is during these periods that adults need to purposefully reflect on the behaviors being modeled.*

Make the Most of the Strategies Through Feedback

If our goal is to model the behaviors we want to elicit in our students, it is critical to be self-aware. The problem is, we don't know what we don't know. The Johari window was developed by psychologists Joseph Luft and Harrington Ingham in the 1950s to help individuals better understand themselves and others.[11] The model illustrates four areas of awareness:

THE JOHARI WINDOW OF COMMUNICATION	Known to Self	Unknown to Self
Known to Others	**1** **Open** Things I know about myself that are also seen and acknowledged by others	**2** **My Blind Spot** Things I don't know about myself but are seen and acknowledged by others
Unknown to Others	**3** **Hidden** Things I know about myself but are not known by others	**4** **Unknown** Things I don't know about myself and are not known by others

Quadrant #1 is considered *open*. The communication flow of information in this section is based on what individuals know about me, as well as what I know about myself. I talk a lot. This is no secret to me or others who know me. We are all aware of this fact.

Quadrant #2 represents a person's *blind spot*. This area represents information individuals know about us but that we don't know about ourselves. Students in your class might be very aware that you always call on certain students to answer questions. However, this might not be something you consciously know of yourself.

Quadrant #3 is considered *hidden*. This section is based on information I know about myself, but others do not. I might have a fear of rodents. I keep this fact to myself, therefore others are unaware of my issue.

Quadrant #4 is considered *unknown*. These are things I, or others, don't know about myself. I might have a natural gift or a talent that has never been tapped. Many of an individual's hidden potentials lie in this quadrant.

When it comes to modeling, quadrant #2 is worth noting. We all have a blind spot when it comes to our own behaviors because we don't see ourselves the way others do. In other words, we don't know what we don't know. Have you ever heard your voice on a recording and thought, *Do I really sound like that?* This is why feedback is so important. As teachers, we need a vehicle for learning about our own behaviors and how they impact others. Consider having a colleague observe you teaching and provide feedback to you. Another option would be to video a lesson you teach and watch it back. Look for ways you can get feedback on your behaviors and the message they send to others through modeling.

At times, relationships are damaged due to teachers' mindsets. "I'll give that student respect when he shows me respect." Unfortunately, some students have not had healthy role models for respect, so they might not know how to give it. It is also important to remember that our students, given their age, have had much less time to learn how to give respect. We give students unconditional respect not based on whether or not the deserve it. We give students respect because by doing so we teach and model the very behaviors we are wanting them to internalize and regularly demonstrate.

CAUTION

In Summary . . .

The behaviors to which students are exposed serve to shape their own behaviors. Family members, peers, teachers, and social media all play a part in this process. The more a pattern of behavior is modeled, the more likely it will be viewed as normal or accepted in the mind of the student. It is for this reason adults in the school setting need to continuously model appropriate behaviors. Our body language, word choice, volume, and tone are all factors impacting student behaviors.

Self-awareness is a critical aspect of modeling. A teacher who has a naturally loud volume level can elicit the same from students if he or she is not aware of this attribute. This is why feedback and reflection are so important. It is in examining our own behaviors in light of this principle that we are best able to be good role models for our students.

FINAL THOUGHT

Experience is the best teacher. By purposefully modeling appropriate behaviors, we increase the chance our students will both internalize and demonstrate them in the future.

Intervention Principles

Since students all have different gifts and challenges, invariably not all students will respond to prevention efforts. The next three principles should be considered when designing interventions for students who need a higher level of behavioral support. These principles should be studied and incorporated, along with the first four designed for prevention. When examining the role of attention, developmental levels, and our behavioral teaching efforts, we are able to put strong strategies in place to hopefully keep these students from dropping into the lower level of this continuum.

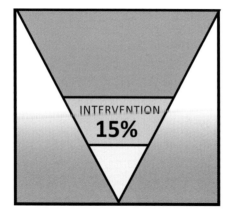

5. **Attention** magnifies behavior.

   The magnifying glass icon represents our point of focus. Attention is a powerful tool for shaping behaviors. However, we have to know how to use it in such a way that it increases positive behaviors and deters negative ones from becoming poor habits.

6. **Developmental levels** influence behaviors.

We all do the best we are able given the skills at our disposal. For some students, the best they are able to do is determined by their social and emotional levels of functioning. When we look at students, we should look beyond their physical age. The silhouette icon reminds us to look beyond our students' physical ages and, instead, meet them at their unique developmental levels.

7. Behaviors are strengthened through **skill development.**

When students have skill deficits, we teach. The same strategy should apply for behavior deficits. When we assume students know how to behave, we miss an opportunity to reinforce appropriate skills and develop them into strong healthy habits. The book icon reminds us to focus on teaching as the primary means of shaping positive behaviors.

Attention Magnifies Behavior

Educators wear many hats. We rotate through committees and are given a great number of responsibilities beyond our primary role of teaching students. Given my experience and training, one consistent job I have carried throughout my career is that of crisis response. I'm a card-carrying member of that group of educators who are called when behaviors escalate to the point of needing outside intervention. When teachers "buzz" the office, we intervene to de-escalate, process the incident, teach replacement behaviors, and reintegrate the student back into the classroom setting. The good news is that this job afforded me the opportunity to see consistent behavior patterns of students exhibited throughout our school. And these patterns helped me understand ways to intervene appropriately—which brings us to our next story.

Runaway

Trent was in second grade when he transferred to our school. He had been receiving support through special education with an Other Health Impairment (OHI), having been diagnosed with ADHD. I called the case manager at his former school to get some history and she provided me a great deal of information. "He wants to please. He wants friends. He likes school. He hates it when teachers buzz the office. He throws things. He will call you names. Oh, and wear tennis shoes to work—he's a runner." "Tell me more," I inquired. It seemed Trent ran out of the classroom and throughout the building when he got in trouble and had been doing so since pre-kindergarten. "It usually takes several people to corral him before being able to get him back to class," she said. This last statement obviously concerned me, but I was equally as troubled that this running behavior had been going on for several years without interruption.

When Trent arrived at our school, we were lucky to have three days of a honeymoon period with no running. When he got upset, he sat under his desk, but the teacher was able to handle the situation in the classroom. By day four, behaviors escalated. Trent ran out of the room and down the hall, and, as anticipated, it took several adults intervening before we were able to get him back to class. These running incidents continued daily for a week, at which time I called a meeting so we could come up with a new plan of support for Trent.

My first suggestion to the committee alarmed the group. "We need to stop running after this child when he leaves the room." Although there are exceptions to the rule, I firmly believe that, for the most part, the reason we have "runners" is because we have "chasers." I was not implying we should let him run away, or not ensure his safety, but we had to acknowledge that our current method of chasing was not improving the situation. Additionally, the running pattern was becoming a habit, and the longer it continued, the harder the habit would be to break.

After some discussion, we implemented a new plan. When Trent left the class, his classroom teacher immediately "buzzed" the office and informed a neighboring teacher of the situation. Someone from the office, coupled with the neighboring teacher, inconspicuously kept Trent in continual sight in order to keep him safe and assure he would not leave the building. However, individuals did not approach or chase him. The goal was to minimize the amount of attention he was receiving when he eloped.

As anticipated, the following day, Trent got upset and ran out of class. He ran down the hall and waited by the stairwell. He kept looking back toward the classroom, waiting for his teacher or someone to come after him, but no one did. After a few minutes he walked back toward his classroom. He stayed right outside the door and popped his head in and out for a few minutes before the teacher calmly approached him. "Hey Trent. We are about to start on journals. Can you help me pass them out?" She didn't wait for an answer, but when she turned to walk back in the classroom, Trent followed and joined in the activity. Later that same day, the teacher circled back around to discuss the incident with Trent and teach him alternatives to leaving the class when he got upset. Trent still exhibited a great number of other behavior concerns, but we were able to extinguish his running behaviors within a few weeks, all due to the simple strategy of not feeding the attention.

Had this been a student who would have run out of the building and into the street, we would have handled the situation differently, but the point of this story is to understand the role of attention when dealing with behavior. Initially Trent was getting a great deal of attention from a lot of adults when he ran, and this response was reinforcing the behavior. By minimizing attention to inappropriate behavior in this incident, we were able to effectively stop it.

"Look at Me"

Trent, like many students, was very skilled at using his inappropriate behaviors to garner attention. Every time he ran, several adults dropped what they were doing and focused on his needs, trying to get him back to class. This pattern was not isolated to running. When he misbehaved in the classroom, students turned and looked at him, as well. His *novel* behaviors became a regular focal point for the class. This cycle is typical with students who need a great deal of behavioral intervention.

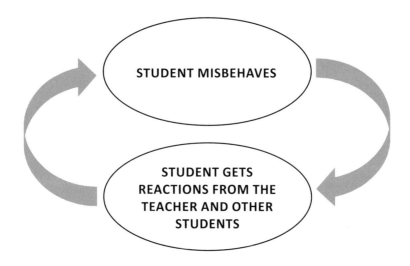

When minor behaviors present themselves in the classroom setting, it is common for teachers to verbally redirect students and extinguish the concerns. However, for some students, the attention garnered through the redirection can actually reinforce the very behaviors teachers are trying to extinguish. "But that makes no sense to me," a teacher once told me. "I understand why a student would want attention like praise, but why on earth would anyone want negative attention?" I explained to her that attention is usually a vehicle helping us meet other needs.

Attention as Belonging

We all have the need to belong. As social beings, we naturally want to connect and be accepted, and attention is a natural vehicle for getting this need met. When we pay attention to someone, a connection is made. A monologue can become a dialogue. Solitude can become an interaction. Some students regularly act out, drawing others into an interaction and feeding their need to belong.

When I first started teaching, I worked in a residential treatment facility. As one of my responsibilities, I worked in the adjustment room—a place where students could go when they needed to calm down. Margaret was one student who frequented the room. The sequence of events leading to her daily visits was fairly consistent: Margaret would misbehave. The teacher would redirect her behavior. Margaret's behaviors would continue to escalate, and eventually she had to be physically escorted to the adjustment room.

I remember one day talking with her about the frequency of her visits. "Margaret, wouldn't you rather be in class?" I asked. "No," she answered emphatically. This was not the response I was looking for. The adjustment room was not supposed to be a place students *wanted* to be. There was an unspoken norm that the adjustment room was designed as negative reinforcement. I expected Margaret to say, "I hate it here. Can I go back to class now?" Nope. Instead, she put her head down and quietly mumbled, "At least here someone talks to me." With this one sentence, I realized that, for Margaret, getting negative attention was better than getting no attention at all.

In analyzing the times Margaret was brought to the adjustment room, we noticed a pattern. Her biggest problems occurred when she was working on group projects, during free periods, and at unstructured times. When a teacher was directing instruction and Margaret did not have to interact with other students, she was fairly successful. However, when she was put in unstructured social situations, Margaret felt isolated and lacked the skills to successfully navigate through interactions. These were the times when she was most at risk for exhibiting problematic behaviors.

When Margaret was brought to the adjustment room, she had a connection with me, as well as with the other students who regularly visited the room. She also had a place. She always sat in the same chair and same cubicle. In looking back at this situation now, I realize to some degree, the adjustment room served as a home for Margaret. It was a place where she felt acceptance, connection, and a sense of belonging. Her one comment helped me understand that she felt more comfortable in our setting than her regular classroom.

Attention as Novelty

Some classrooms are a breeding ground for misbehavior due to a lack of novelty in instructional methods. When students

> *In the absence of instructional engagement, behavioral engagement settles in.*

are in classroom environments steeped in strong *rituals* of direct instruction, small amounts of misbehavior can easily become the novelty on which other students focus. And sadly, some students' behavioral problems are very engaging, to say the least. In the absence of instructional engagement, *behavioral engagement* settles in.

Attention As Power and Control

We all need some degree of control in our lives to feel safe. Unfortunately, some students are unable to control many factors in their lives: divorced parents, poor social relations, erratic schedules of sleep. A natural inclination in this situation is unconscious compensation—"If I don't have control in this area of my life, I'll take control by commanding negative attention." In my opinion, students with more chronic and severe behaviors are more apt to get into power struggles with others, and by doing so, they feed their need for attention. Unfortunately, the more adults inadvertently perpetuate the power struggles, the more we are reinforcing the undesired behaviors.

The Dangers of Negative Attention: Criticism Rituals

When students receive continual negative attention, a danger is that their undesirable behaviors will develop into habits. This is a common situation for students who have behavioral difficulties. They unconsciously seek what they are used to receiving: negative attention. Their inappropriate behaviors invite criticism from others and, over time, they get comfortable with negative feedback, partially due to the fact that this is all they know. Unfortunately, this type of continual attention damages relationships and destroys trust over time. Additionally, when individuals hear the same negative comments over and over again (rituals), they unconsciously tune them out.

Early in my teaching, I got into a particularly nasty power struggle with one of my high school students, Jim. When we sat down afterward to work through the problem, I recreated a timeline of the incident. As we mapped out what happened, I was surprised by Jim's inability to articulate, or even remember, most of the details. At the end of our discussion, I recall apologizing to Jim for having raised my voice in anger. His response to me still sticks with me to this day. He looked at me and said, "It's okay, Mr. St. Romain. It's not a big deal. I'm used to it." My emotional response was one of both understanding and sadness.

The Dangers of Negative Attention: Shut-Down Mode

I realized Jim had developed what I termed a *criticism ritual*. He was so used to getting yelled at and criticized that he became numb to the feedback. He seemed to have an automatic shut-down response when confronted by his behavior. I guessed this was why he couldn't remember the details of the event. During the incident, he unconsciously tuned adults out and went into survival mode. In the face of repeated negative interactions, the brain shuts down.

Think About It . . .

Students aren't the only ones who shut down in the face of repeated criticism and negative attention. When teachers continually draw attention to students' behavior problems, parents find ways to avoid receiving it as well. Phone calls from the school don't get answered; behavior folders don't get checked; conferences don't get attended. If we don't want parents to get into the habit of avoiding communication with us, we have to refrain from providing continual negative feedback.

The Dangers of Negative Attention: The Ripple Effect

A teacher's natural instinct is to redirect a student who is misbehaving so they don't lose that child's attention. A bigger concern classroom teachers face is losing the attention of the rest of the students while attending to the one who is misbehaving. When this happens, a ripple effect is created. It starts with one student, and then, one by one, others join in and, within minutes, the whole class is out of control. Every teacher has had this "herding ants at a picnic" experience. Teachers play behavioral whack-a-mole to the point of exhaustion.

In looking at this problem a different way, when a student misbehaves, teachers often focus their attention on the student with the most extreme behavioral concerns (5 percent of the class), and by doing so, they draw attention away from instruction and toward misbehavior. When this happens and goes uninterrupted, more students jump on the misbehavior bandwagon (15 percent of the class). At this point, if the cycle is not broken, the rest of the class (the remaining 80 percent) begins to engage in the same negative behaviors, all continually losing focus on instruction.

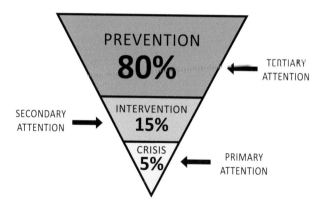

This behavioral ripple effect is a common occurance in classrooms. The good news is that this cycle can be interrupted and reversed if we implement effective strategies based on this principle.

Strategies for Providing Attention

Attention is a very powerful behavior management tool. When teachers understand the nature of attention, they can implement strategies designed to decrease the likelihood of behavior problems being amplified in the classroom. Let's walk through several simple ways to take advantage of this principle.

Draw Attention Away from Misbehavior, Rather than Toward It

A common recommended behavioral strategy is to use proximity control to stop inappropriate behavior: "When students misbehave while you are teaching, walk by their desks and stand by them." Although this can be an effective strategy for minor misbehaviors, when dealing with students who have more extreme behaviors, this strategy can actually make the behaviors worse. Standing next to a student only serves to draw more attention to the inappropriate behaviors.

Drawing attention *away* from the misbehavior seems counterintuitive; however, if we look at attention as power, the goal should be to diminish the amount of power a student receives for negative behaviors rather than feeding it. Since the brain can only consciously attend to one thing at a time, when a disruption in class occurs, look for ways to focus the attention of students elsewhere. Walk in the opposite direction of the student or problem and couple it with a specific phrase directing attention away from the misbehavior. "Look at what I'm holding in my hand. Raise your hand if you can name three of its attributes." By giving the students a specific focal point for their attention, they have to choose to attend either to the misbehavior or to your prompt, the latter of which is the goal.

PERSPECTIVE *SHIFT*

Drawing attention away from misbehavior requires a change in perspective and practice for teachers, which can be difficult. Although the principle advocates drawing attention away from misbehavior, this does not mean teachers shouldn't redirect minor behavior concerns. Redirection in the context of a healthy relationship between the teacher and student is appropriate. The concern arises when a student is continually being redirected. In this case, it is better to draw attention away from the misbehavior and redirect privately in a way that provides the student with your expectations while also keeping a healthy relationship intact.

Reverse the Ripple Effect

> *The more students are attending to you and instruction, the fewer you will have attending to and feeding the negative behaviors of others in the classroom.*

When a student begins to misbehave, our goal should be to reverse the ripple effect, with the tide moving away from misbehavior rather than toward it. The first step in accomplishing this is to secure the attention of the 80-percent group of students—or the majority of the class. As the saying goes, "There is power in numbers." The more students are attending to you and instruction, the fewer you will have attending to and feeding the negative behaviors of others in the classroom.

Once you have secured the attention of the majority of the students in your classroom (80 percent), then target the followers (15 percent). Using eye contact, interactive teaching methods, and distraction, work to pull the attention of these students away from the misbehavior. The goal is to put the students in the classroom in a position to have to make a conscious choice between attending to you or to the students who are misbehaving. As discussed, behaviors mainly occur in a relationship. The more we are able to interrupt the interaction of the students misbehaving, the less attention behaviors receive and the more likely they will begin to diminish.

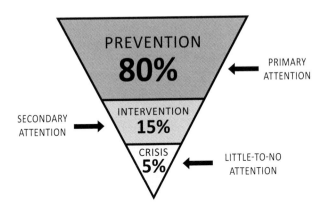

To the best of our ability we should avoid providing any attention to the students who are misbehaving. Our goal is to draw the class's attention away from those students so they do not inadvertently feed the primary negative behaviors. We wait until the misbehaviors subside before jumping in and providing attention. Obviously, we have to redirect or prompt if it is a crisis situation where safety is concerned, but with less severe behaviors, planned ignoring is key.

Provide Attention in the Form of More Encouragement and Less Criticism

Students who exhibit behavior problems are used to getting a great deal of attention from adults in the form of negative feedback:

"Michael, stop doing that."

"Son, pay attention."

"I'm not going to tell you again. You need to listen."

These comments, when heard continuously, become *rituals* of sound that the students unconsciously tune out. If our goal is to strengthen positive behaviors, the best way to combat this problem is to provide less ritualized criticism and more *novel* comments in the form of positive feedback. Praise and encouragement will always be a better method for improving behaviors than criticism, whatever the behaviors might be.

> *Praise and encouragement will always be a better method for improving behaviors than criticism . . .*

Note: Just as students respond better to praise and encouragement, so do parents. Look for ways to provide positive feedback to parents about their child. By looking for opportunities to acknowledge students' positive choices, we not only draw attention to the behaviors we want, but we also ultimately strengthening our relationships with the parents in the process.

Direct Attention Using Interactive Teaching Methods and a Higher Degree of Novelty

As noted in the second Positive Behavior Principle, novelty focuses attention. The more we are able to infuse novelty into our teaching, the more we are able to focus attention on instruction, which is our ultimate goal. Use callbacks, interactive reviews, gestures, and other novel approaches to keep students actively engaged in the learning process. When students get into the habit of being an active part of the lesson rather than the passive recipient of a lecture-based classroom, it becomes much easier for you as the teacher to draw their attention away from students who are misbehaving. Additionally, when your direct teach pieces are shorter and students are working more on group projects and other interactive self-directed activities, you are freed up to work with individual students who might need redirection in a more direct way. When students are attending to their self-directed work, you can provide this redirection in a more private way.

Make Eye Contact—"I See You"

Eye contact is a powerful tool for attention. Get into the habit of using purposeful eye contact with all students. Not only does this strategy model a good social skill, but it also allows you to use eye contact to secure attention. When dealing with milder behavior issues like a side discussion, making eye contact with the students will usually fix the problem. However, with students who have more disruptive behaviors, sometimes the best strategy is to avoid making any eye contact with them at all. Rather, engage the attention of the other students, making eye contact with them individually. When we have the attention of the other students, and strategically avoid eye contact with the student exhibiting the problem, negative behaviors are more likely to fade.

When using eye contact, how we give it is as important as when and how often we use it. Our facial expression, body language, and tone all contribute to how eye contact is received. The goal is for the eye contact to engage the attention of the student, not to embarrass. When teachers use eye contact consistently throughout their teaching, it is easier to naturally use it as a tool for curtailing off-task behaviors. However, if eye contact is not used regularly, when a teacher does look at a student who is misbehaving, that individual often feels singled out. Eye contact moves from a place of healthy engagement to becoming "the look," which is what we want to avoid.

> *The goal is for the eye contact to engage the attention of the student, not to embarrass.*

Eric Jensen, a leader in the field of education, often says, "The best discipline is the kind nobody notices."[12] This is our goal with eye contact. When used purposefully and consistently, eye contact can be a very effective tool for redirection without any students being aware the strategy was even used.

Teach "Attention Avoidance"

All classrooms encounter regular disruptions to the learning environment. Be proactive with students and teach them strategies of avoidance. If a disruptive student is escorted out of the classroom, take the time to coach the other students by saying something like, "Michael was very angry. When you are angry, what do you want? I want to be left alone. I also don't like it when people look at me. Let's talk about ways, as a class, we can help Michael if this happens again." These teachable moments are very important strategies for directing attention away from negative behaviors when they arise. These discussions also go a long way in teaching the other students to be more empathetic with their classmates and less judgmental.

In some classes, especially in the primary grades, popular behavior management programs demand a lot of attention. Teachers spend a lot of time managing behavior folders, clip systems, Class Dojo, and other reward- and punishment-based systems. These methods draw a whole lot of attention to both positive and negative behaviors. Since attention magnifies behavior, we might want to reevaluate our methods. If we really want students attending to instruction, we should question putting behavioral systems in place that draw attention away from it.

CAUTION

In Summary . . .

Traditional discipline methods often rely on bringing attention to misbehavior as a means of discouraging it. Public redirection and use of proximity are classic examples. These interventions can be effective in stopping minor disruptive behaviors when used sparingly in the context of healthy relationships. However, these methods can also inadvertently escalate behaviors, as well as damage relationships between the students and teachers. This is especially the case when working with students who have more challenging behaviors. Rather than verbally pointing out misbehavior, a more effective intervention is to draw students' attention away from the problem. By doing so, the inappropriate behavior is not inadvertently strengthened. As less attention is given to inappropriate behaviors, they will be more likely to subside.

FINAL THOUGHT

Attention is a powerful tool that can be used to shape behaviors when we purposefully direct it toward desired ones and away from those we hope to discourage.

PRINCIPLE
SIX

Developmental Levels
Influence Behaviors

It would be an understatement to say that among
students with behavioral concerns there is a large gender
disproportionality. Need a bit of proof? Call to mind
several students over the years with whom you have
had behavioral difficulties. Next, make a list of your top
five. My guess is that the majority are males. For further
proof, one only needs to look at office referrals, detention
rosters, and alternative schools to notice the large gender
disproportionality across all grade levels between males
and females with behavior infractions. If we look at the
2018–19 school year in Colorado, for example, we find
that male students represented a much larger percentage
of disciplinary actions than female students. Male students
made up 78.15 percent of classroom removals, 74.57
percent of in-school suspensions, 73.05 percent of out-
of-school suspensions, and 75.52 percent of expulsions.[13]
Though there are many factors potentially impacting this
discrepancy, I believe maturity and development are key
among them.

"They Don't Understand"

Hands down, it was one of my favorite years of teaching. As part of my school responsibilities, I was asked to present social skill lessons in the fifth-grade classes each month. This is an exciting time for students as they move into the upper grades, but the transition years from elementary to secondary status can also be quite difficult. This is probably why I was asked to work with six students in a small group setting who needed extra support. Each of these students had been identified by their teachers as having behavioral difficulties and, not surprisingly, all were males.

The list of concerns from the classroom teachers was fairly consistent. All six young men had trouble following directions, paying attention, and staying on task, so their behaviors frequently disrupted the learning environment. The teachers were most concerned that the students' behaviors were significantly interfering with their academic progress, as evidenced by work not being completed or returned.

In my first session with the students, I quickly discovered all of these boys had a few things in common. They all seemed younger and more immature than one would expect from students at this age, they all made silly comments, and they all had great difficulty attending to my instructions. It was for this reason I ran the group as I would have with younger students. I gave more prompts. I broke down directions. I provided more guidance. And because I looked at their behaviors through a younger developmental lens, it was easier for me to be more understanding and patient with them.

When we met for our second session, several of the teachers asked me if, in addition to working on the behavior concerns, I could get them to turn in missing assignments. In working with the students during that session, I uncovered several problems:

- Though the students all had agendas, they did not know how to use them.
- Though the students had folders for their assignments, the folders were empty.
- All students had one giant stack of papers comprised of many subjects and incomplete assignments.
- The students' desks all looked like a communal episode of *Hoarders*. When one item was removed, piles of papers and clutter spilled out onto the floor.

These students had organizational problems.

When I talked to the teachers about my discovery, they were not surprised in the least. They concurred but also told me that, as fifth graders, the boys needed to be responsible enough to develop proper work habits on their own. "Dan, next year the sixth-grade teachers aren't going to check their agendas each day. The students need to do it themselves." This is when I had an aha moment. The teachers were expecting the students to behave and act like fifth graders, when in reality these boys demonstrated organizational skills more in line with third or fourth graders. Behavior was not the issue; organizational immaturity was the issue.

Once I started teaching the students how to organize their materials and schedules, their behaviors started to improve as well, but I had to work with them as I would have younger students. I took into consideration the students' young behaviors and acknowledged the role development played in shaping of their behaviors. This helped me design appropriate strategies and ultimately help the students find success.

Developmental Biases

I get it. The fifth-grade teachers were frustrated. They were working hard to help their students transition successfully into the middle school years with the academic skills needed for success. Unfortunately, the boys I worked with made the teachers' jobs more difficult. Though I know the students in my group needed some behavioral support, these teachers had developmental biases which contributed to the problem. As teachers, they were expecting students to act their age—and therein lay the problem.

The process of development unfolds over a lifetime, and although there are some predictable indicators at various stages, each person moves through the timeline at a different pace. Unfortunately, in the school system, where students are grouped by their physical ages, we are not always understanding or accepting of developmental differences, and two unconscious societal norms contribute to the problem: destination and speed.

Destination: Grow up!

In his book, *The 7 Habits of Highly Effective People*, Stephen Covey famously taught us to begin with the end in mind.[14] Visualize the end result of what you want in the future and use that to motivate you to work toward accomplishing the goal in the present. Although this is a great practice, the danger of focusing on the future is that we miss out on the present. Put another way, when we overly focus on the end product or result of what we want, we can inadvertently undervalue the process of getting there. I find adults often do this with children, and teachers do it with their students. We see where we want them to be and, thus, become impatient about giving them the time and development needed to get there. Ironically, it is allowing our kids to experience the bumps along the way that will help them learn from their mistakes and best grow into the people we ultimately want them to be.

Speed: Hurry up!

Fast is good; slow is bad—or at least that is the message kids are internalizing at a young age, courtesy of current pop culture and societal norms. Be it fast cars, fast food, or fast internet, we place a high importance on speed. The quicker, the better. We value speed because we value time. The more quickly we accomplish something, the more quickly we can move on to the next thing. So it is only natural that adults unintentionally put this expectation on kids. Not only do we want children to grow up, we want them to do it quickly.

Unfortunately, as a dad, I was guilty of having this mindset of destination and speed with my children. "When are they going to grow up?" I knew what I wanted from them, and I was frustrated that their behaviors were not matching my expectations. Of course, the fault in this

. . . we can't force development. line of reasoning is that we can't force development. It plays out on its own timetable, and attempts to speed up the process simply create frustration. Additionally, I learned as a dad that just because our kids grow physically older, that doesn't mean other areas of development follow suit as quickly.

Developmental Lags

I remember the day vividly. My second-born son was in middle school when one of his elementary teachers asked me a simple question. "How old is Micah now?" I was just about to answer her when I had a revelation. "'How old is Micah,' you ask? Well, that depends. Age is relative."

Physical Development – How old am I?

A person's physical development is a large category encompassing age, size, fine and gross motor skills, and other attributes, but for the purposes of this information, when we refer to an individual's physical development, we are more often than not referring to their physical age.

Cognitive Development – Do I understand this?

Cognition is the ability of a person to acquire knowledge and understanding through thought and experience. When referring to cognitive development, we are usually talking about intelligence. This is the area of development primarily focused on the school system.

At times, behavior concerns stem from cognitive concerns. As one high school student told me, "Mr. St. Romain, I talked back to the teacher because she kept embarrassing me. She always calls on me when I don't know the answer, and no one wants to look stupid." Fear of embarrassment and failure can be strong contributing factors to inappropriate behaviors.

Social Development – Can I get along with you?

Do you know a person with poor social skills? Social skills have to do with our ability to appropriately interact with other individuals. In the school setting, social skills for students can take the form of peer-to-peer or peer-to-adult interactions. Some students are comfortable interacting with adults but not peers. Others might do fine with peers who are younger, but they struggle with age-appropriate peers. Still others might have difficulty with authority figures, and therefore, don't accept directions from adults well. Knowing a student's skill level with regard to their social development provides a great deal of insight into their behaviors.

Emotional Development – Can I hold it together?

Emotional development has to do with our ability to inhibit or exhibit our feelings appropriately. Things don't always turn out the way we want or expect, and the way we handle these disappointments provides a good window into understanding a person's emotional development—the goal being that we all handle frustrations in a positive, adaptive way. Unfortunately, many individuals manifest their feelings in unhealthy ways, shutting down or closing off (imploding) or lashing out (exploding) at others.

Ethical Development – Do I do the right thing?

At a very basic level, ethical development could be defined as an understanding of right and wrong and the ability to make good choices accordingly. Though the process of ethical development unfolds over a large span of time, the frontal lobes of the cerebral cortex, which process reasoning and good judgement, don't fully develop until individuals are in their mid-twenties.[15] Given the lateness in which this development occurs, it would be reasonable to expect younger individuals to make poor choices as they work through this process.

Each of these areas of development will have an impact on the behavior of an individual. Take my son Micah as an example. When he was in sixth grade Micah was *physically* twelve years old. Though at the time he was one of the oldest students in his class, Micah looked physically younger due to his small size and stature. *Cognitively*, however, he presented himself as an older student. Learning came easily for Micah, so he was placed in advanced classes. Unfortunately, organizational issues negatively impacted his ability to take advantage of his strong cognition. Additionally, Micah could do the work presented but often chose not to because he wanted to do something else. In terms of *social* and *emotional* development, Micah demonstrated behaviors typical of a younger child. His social interactions were immature, and he had a difficult time regulating his emotional state when things didn't go the way he wanted them to. As a result of his young social and emotional behaviors, *ethically* he had poor judgement and, at times, made some unfortunate choices. Micah had very asynchronous development, and, as a result, his uneven rates of maturation strongly impacted his behavior.

Fast-forward over a decade and Micah matured. His differing developmental levels more closely aligned and, in essence, he "grew up." Time and natural development provided Micah the skills he needed to work through the incongruence of his cognitive, social, and emotional ages.

In looking back over his history, I feel confident that Micah's varying developmental levels were at the root of his behavior concerns. Fortunately, Micah was able to make it through some turbulent years and, thanks to a variety of factors, come out on the other side functioning well. The same cannot be said for all kids with developmental age discrepancies.

Ageism Redefined – the Unspoken Bias

It can be frustrating for adults when kids present themselves as emotionally or socially young. This is especially the case for teachers. When we have a room full of students with similar physical ages, we set an unspoken standard of expectation for behavior. You can hear the concern in the words we use:

- The other students don't do that.
- He needs to grow up.
- That's not something a high school student does.
- I'm not going to baby him. He needs to figure it out.

Although it is normal to have expectations based on what is typical, problems arise when teachers have one set of behavioral standards for all students. When we fail to differentiate in giving students the support they need to be socially and emotionally successful, we increase

> *Just as we differentiate instructional practices, so should we differentiate the support we offer students based on their developmental levels.*

students' frustration levels and inadvertently make problems worse. Just as we differentiate instructional practices, so should we differentiate the support we offer students based on their developmental levels.

The Bigger the Gap, the Stronger the Frustration

Teachers of young children understand that some students start school with young social and emotional behaviors. They expect to help their students learn friendship and conflict resolution skills. They know their students have had differing amounts of experience with school and social interactions. Put another way, atypically young behaviors in the primary grades are expected and developmentally appropriate. For this reason, teachers' tolerance levels for dealing with these behaviors are usually high. However, as students move through the grade levels and get older, behaviors settle out. This makes students who move along the social and emotional developmental maturation scale at a slower rate stand out. Additionally, as students get older, teachers' expectations are raised and tolerance levels are lowered. The bigger the gap between physical age and young social and emotional ages, the more frustrated teachers often get.

Strategies for Taking into Consideration Developmental Levels

Though we can't force individuals to "grow up," there are strategies we can implement that will help our students move through the developmental process more easily. These strategies also serve to remind us of the impact of development on behavior, hopefully helping us become less frustrated with our students when behavior problems invariably surface.

Informally Assess Social-Emotional Learning (SEL)

There is no set evaluation for determining various stages of development; however, most teachers have a good understanding of developmentally appropriate expectations for the age of students with whom they work. By observing students, we can get a good idea of emotional development based on how they handle frustration when things don't go their way. Additionally, we can observe their interaction with others to learn about their social skills.

Provide Opportunities for Social Interaction

Kids of all ages need basic social skills. Just as we want our students to be academically literate, it is just as critical for students to be socially literate and have strong skills in interacting with others. When we encourage opportunities for students to interact with peers during instruction, we are able to provide a natural venue for these skills to be strengthened.

Help Students Identify and Understand Their Emotional States

Feelings trigger many behaviors that cause behavior problems in the classroom setting. Unfortunately, many students bottle up their feelings and don't learn how to express frustrations appropriately. By actively teaching students about their emotional states, we can help them learn how to channel the feelings and express them in appropriate ways. This is especially important in the primary grades, as well as during the teenage years when hormones are raging and being expressed through behaviors.

Strengthen Relationships – Ethical Development

If we want students to develop an ethical conscience and make good choices, it is important to foster healthy relationships. When students develop healthy relationships, they develop concern for others. Concern for others leads to empathy. Empathy strengthens ethical development. We want students to understand that their behaviors and choices impact others. By working to strengthen peer-to-peer relationships, along with peer-to-adult relationships, we increase the likelihood that students will make good choices out of concern for others. This goes a long way in helping students develop an ethical conscience.

RELATIONSHIP ➡ EMPATHY ➡ CONCERN FOR OTHERS ➡ ETHICAL DEVELOPMENT

Meet Students at Their Levels (BZPD)

Once we identify students who have developmental lags, to the best of our ability we should try to meet them where they are functioning. This does not mean we coddle or enable them; it simply means we give them the proper level of support needed. Lev Vygotsky taught us about working within a student's zone of proximal development (ZPD).[16] The ZPD refers to what a student is able to do with and without help. When we meet students at their behavioral level, we must individualize support as a way of instructing them within their behavioral zone of proximal development (BZPD). We want students to be challenged based on their current level of functioning but not so frustrated that they lash out or give up. Just as we differentiate academic support for students, so should we differentiate the behavioral support afforded to students based on their developmental levels across the continuum. We provide behavioral accommodations based on what they need to be successful.

PERSPECTIVE *SHIFT*

Can you recall making some very unfortunate choices when you were in high school? Most of us can. However, the choices we made led to consequences which not only shaped our future choices but also helped spur our development along in many areas. Experience is often the best teacher, as well as an influencing factor that helps encourage maturity. Although we can't force development, we can allow time and natural experiences to strengthen maturity in a variety of developmental areas.

Give Students Responsibilities

When students are put in leadership roles, they have the opportunity to develop skills that encourage maturation. Find simple ways to give students responsibilities through classroom jobs and projects. Have students take roll, lead activities, be a peer tutor, etc. Responsibilities will foster independence, which is a critical life skill needed for healthy development in a number of areas.

Be Patient

Development unfolds on its own course and we can't rush the process. This means we must be patient. Just as it takes some students a great deal of time before they master academic concepts, so, too, will others need additional time before they mature socially and emotionally. When maturation levels settle out, we want students to have healthy trusting relationships with us.

This is more likely to happen if adults are tolerant and understanding while our students are still working through this developmental process.

Shift Your Perspective

Perhaps the most important strategy to take into consideration with this principle is to shift perspectives. When we try to understand behavior through the lens of developmental stages, we can be more empathetic and less judgmental. When able, I find it helpful to approach behavior from the idea that we all do the best we are able, given our developmental levels and skill sets. As developmental levels rise and skill sets strengthen, so too will student behaviors improve—and no amount of nagging or punishment will help this happen any quicker.

This principle advocates meeting students at their developmental levels. **CAUTION** Some educators have a difficult time philosophically with doing this, as they believe that it enables coddling the student. Just as we modify to meet students' academic needs, so, too, should we modify to meet their behavioral needs. Adapting expectations based on needs is just good teaching practice. If

Just as we modify to meet students' academic needs, so, too, should we modify to meet their behavioral needs.

we don't provide some wiggle room for maturation, students might implode or explode out of frustration, which is a far greater problem in the long run than simply adjusting our behavioral expectations.

In Summary . . .

Although inappropriate behaviors are often due to poor choices on the part of the student, problems can also be the result of developmental lags in one or more areas:

- **Emotional** – Our ability to inhibit or exhibit our feelings appropriately
- **Social** – Our ability to get along and interact with others
- **Ethical** – Our ability to understand right from wrong and make good choices
- **Cognitive** – Our intellectual capacity
- **Physical** – Our physical growth and development, coupled with our age

Our abilities in each of these areas of development directly influence our actions, so this information must be taken into account when attempting to understand behavior and design appropriate intervention.

As students get older, teachers naturally have higher behavioral expectations for them. We expect students to "act their age." However, our chronological age is not always the same as our social or emotional age. Many high school teachers, for example, can identify students who display "middle school" social behaviors. When supporting behavior, all developmental ages should be taken into consideration.

FINAL THOUGHT

By understanding how developmental levels impact behavior, we are in a better position to adjust our perspectives, be more patient with students, and target interventions accordingly.

Positive Behavior Principles

PRINCIPLE
SEVEN

Behaviors Are Strengthened Through Skill Development

Let's be honest, some jobs are harder than others. As a special education teacher, working predominately in behavior settings, I've always known my job would be a challenge. However, I believe there are other positions in education I would find infinitely more difficult. At the top of the list are bus drivers, substitute teachers, lunchroom monitors, and detention/in-school suspension (ISS) coordinators. There are exceptions to the rule, but given the job responsibilities involved, individuals who fill these positions usually work with a large number of students and have less time to develop individual relationships with them. I find this combination of limitations difficult. If I had to choose one of these positions, I would want to work with students placed in detention or in-school suspension. However, I would run my program differently than most. My job responsibilities would have to be altered.

"They Never Learn"

Several years back, I was hired as a consultant for a small school district needing behavioral support. There was a high number of students receiving special education services who were being placed in ISS, and the district had been charged by the State Department of Education to make some changes. My job was to observe the ISS settings throughout the district and make recommendations based on my findings.

During my time there, I observed at different schools, spoke with the ISS coordinators and classroom teachers, talked with a few students, and looked at the discipline referral data. Several common themes emerged:

- The majority of students in ISS were repeat offenders.
- Most students were assigned to ISS for a fixed amount of time (half, whole, or multiple days).
- The students either slept or worked silently on classwork during their time in ISS.
- At the high school, the students were expected to copy parts of the school's code of conduct before returning to class.
- The on-campus administrators processed the referrals and talked with the students, but the ISS coordinator's job was simply to monitor the room when students were present. Aside from intermittent redirection, the ISS coordinators had minimal interactions with the students.

Prior to making recommendations, I sat down with staff from the central office and asked them to talk with me about the goal of the ISS program. Their main objective, they stated, was to improve student behaviors, but given their number of repeat offenders, the methods being used to accomplish this goal did not seem to be effective. "It's sad. We see the same students over and over. It seems like they never learn," said one administrator. *I couldn't have said it better myself*, I thought. "If the goal is for the students to learn appropriate behaviors," I said, "instruction is needed. So, my suggestion would be to concentrate less on punishing and spend a great deal more time teaching appropriate behaviors during ISS."

After having a lengthy discussion with the staff, I was able to better understand the problem. Their ISS strategies were based on a mindset of punishment. The unspoken beliefs were that:

- Students were in ISS because they made poor choices.
- If they wanted to, the students could make good choices.
- To avoid future punishment, students will make better choices.

The problem with this line of reasoning is that it does not take into consideration other factors that might be contributing to the behavior problems beyond choice:

- Poor impulse control
- Developmental immaturity
- Neurological issues

- Deficit social skills
- Deeply ingrained poor behavioral habits

This line of thought is also based on the assumption that punishment works. However, in this case, the informal data of the number of repeat offenders clearly indicated otherwise. Their interventions were not working. Research would support this claim. Traditional punishments relying on compliance-based negative reinforcement usually only serves to escalate student conflicts and fuel power struggles.[17] In order for this district to move forward in a positive direction, a change in both philosophy and practice was needed. Discipline efforts needed to focus on teaching and practicing appropriate behavioral skills rather than punitive measures.

Moving Past Punishments and Rewards

Most discipline programs in schools are based on traditional models of using punishments and rewards to improve student behaviors. In-school suspension, detention, ClassDoJo, clip systems, token economy systems, and prize boxes are common examples of these methods across the grade levels. Though commonly used, there are several problems with these types of strategies:

External Control

Punishments and rewards are based on external methods used to shape behavior. "If you don't . . . , I will . . . ." We dole out behavior tickets, detention slips, and other tangible means, but the problem with the use of punishments and rewards is that they don't teach self-regulation. They are dependent on others to enforce them. Unfortunately, adults won't always be around to do so. If we want students to make good choices in our absence, the choice has to be made to do so by the students themselves.

External Motivation

We don't want students to make good choices because of fear of punishment or expectation of reward. We want them to do the right thing because they want to do the right thing. Put another way, external punishments and rewards do not create long-term internal motivation for students to make the right choices.

Absence of Teaching

When behavior problems occur, our goal should be to teach students appropriate behaviors, accordingly. However, unless coupled with other strategies, most traditional punishment and reward systems do not teach alternative behaviors; they simply expect them. There is an unspoken assumption that students know the right behaviors and, given the right amount of negative or positive reinforcement, will simply make better choices.

Behaviors are strengthened through skill development. And rather than relying on external methods to shape behaviors, we should utilize strategies that encourage self-regulation. Ultimately, these factors will better prepare students to deal with the inevitable problems they will face after they have left the education system. This, of course, is our goal.

Our Ultimate Goals

Each year we ask the same question to the parents of our students entering kindergarten: *What hopes and dreams do you have for your child?* The responses are fairly consistent:

I hope my child will . . .

- be happy and well-adjusted
- have friends and get along with other people
- be a life-long learner
- make good choices
- dream big

Just to balance out the scales, I ask this question to parents of middle and high school students as well. I receive the same answers as above, but some additional ones surface:

I hope my child will . . .

- be a productive citizen
- make a good living
- be independent and self-sufficient
- contribute to society
- have integrity and be a good person

As a dad, I can relate to all of these answers. They are goals I would imagine every parent would want for their child. When asking parents "What hopes and dreams do you have for your child?" these are answers I don't hear:

I hope my child . . .

- passes the state mandated test
- makes a high ACT or SAT score
- does well on his yearly benchmarks
- gets into the right college

Although this last set of goals is important to some degree, they focus on short-term goals, not long-term hopes and dreams. They also focus solely on cognition. These are goals schools focus on, which is ironic considering the overwhelming majority of hopes and dreams parents have for their children focus on social, emotional, and ethical aspects of development. It is natural that a school's primary focus is cognitive development; however, if we don't contextualize intelligence within a framework of healthy behavioral development, we will fail to help our students actualize the long-term potential in a meaningful way.

> *. . . if we don't contextualize intelligence within a framework of healthy behavioral development, we will fail to help our students actualize the long-term potential in a meaningful way.*

Think About It . . .

Let's put it another way. Look over the list below of common reasons why adults get fired from their jobs. How many of the reasons have to do with cognition? How many are connected to social, emotional, or ethical issues?

- *Lying*
- *Stealing*
- *Poor Performance*
- *Social Media Violation*
- *Insubordination*
- *Harassment*

- *Drugs or Alcohol*
- *Conflicts with Coworkers/Authority*
- *Late/Excessive Absence*
- *Personal Problems*

A Teacher Teaches

At the risk of stating the obvious, a teacher's primary job is to teach and prepare students for life outside the school system. Given common reasons why adults get fired from their jobs, it would seem reasonable that more emphasis would be placed on teaching social and emotional skills in schools.

Though there has been a surge in schools proactively teaching social and emotional learning strategies, interventions for behavioral problems are still mostly rooted in traditional punishments rather than teaching efforts. If we want students *learning* appropriate behaviors, we must move beyond a model of punishment and focus our interventions on *teaching*.

> *If we want students learning appropriate behaviors, we must move beyond a model of punishment and focus our interventions on teaching.*

Core Skills

In working with students as an interventionist across all grade levels, I have found that there is a core set of behavioral skills that seems to surface when called on to provide behavioral support for students. It would seem logical for ISS and detention settings to focus on teaching and reinforcing these skills. If behavior deficits are the reasons students end up in these punishment-based settings, behavioral instruction should be a logical response for getting them out.

Though these skills are highlighted under the intervention principles section of this body of work, all students could benefit from proactive instruction in these areas. The teaching of these skills should not be isolated, meaning they shouldn't be just "one more thing" crammed into an already full schedule. The idea is to integrate them into all areas, referenced and practiced contextually throughout the day as opportunities present themselves.

Following Directions

This is probably the most common social skill referenced in the school system. There is both a cognitive and social component to this skill. Students need to know both how to follow directions (cognitive) and how to work with others following the directions they are given (social).

Unfortunately, we are all getting a bit less practice following directions as advancements in technology are made. Directions are simplified. Steps are more automated and less manual. This trend was summed up in a recent online review for a product I considered purchasing: "Set-up was easy. It was really a no-brainer."

Paying Attention

"He never pays attention." This is a common phrase uttered in classrooms across the country. Unfortunately, more and more students seem to be lacking this social skill. This is evidenced by the alarming rise in the number of students being diagnosed with ADHD due to issues of inattention. I believe this skill deficit is, to some degree, the result of societal conditioning. As discussed in an earlier chapter, when we are conditioned to attend to higher degrees of novelty, attending to less exciting activities becomes more difficult. Advancements in technology require less concentrated attention, as well.

I was recently reminded of the impact of technology on attention spans when I took my wife's van to the grocery store. I had barely left our house when another driver honked at me. Apparently, I wasn't paying attention well enough, as I tried to change lanes and almost cut the other car off. Of course, I blamed the problem on my wife's vehicle. Several years ago, I purchased a new vehicle with fancy lane assist and braking technology. If I try to change lanes and another car is in the way, my vehicle beeps at me. My wife's van, however, doesn't have this technology. Fortunately for her, she is conditioned to pay greater attention while driving. Me? I'm used to my vehicle doing the work for me.

That trip also taught me how in many cases paying attention is less about choice and more about conditioning. When I was driving my wife's van, I wasn't choosing to pay less attention; my brain had just been conditioned to do so. I believe this is what happens to many students in school. They attend to something at first; however, their brains are conditioned to do so for short amounts of time, so they get easily distracted by other more novel activities. They pay attention initially, but sustaining attention becomes the challenge afterward.

Getting Attention Appropriately

Based on our need to belong, we all have a need for attention. Unfortunately, face-to-face attention is becoming increasingly harder to come by. With more single-parent families and caregivers working longer hours, kids are receiving less individual attention from adults than they once did.

As a dad, I learned this lesson firsthand. One of my boys continually went to his friends to discuss issues because I was at work and not around to give him the individual attention he so desperately needed. Trust me, the last thing we want is for one teenager to ask another teenager for advice on serious issues, rather than getting the needed attention and advice from an adult.

Getting attention usually manifests in two ways. One aspect of getting attention is when a person wants to say something. The typical social convention of getting attention in this situation is to wait until another person has finished speaking before interjecting a thought. In school, however, as in many other group settings, the social convention is to raise a hand to get attention. Either way, the skill needs to be taught and practiced.

Respecting Personal Space

Most individuals know adults who do not understand the concept of personal space. As you talk with them, they get too close. You back up in response, but alas, they inch closer. This give-and-take exchange continues until, at last, you step behind a table to force them to give you the personal space you are comfortable with.

The umbrella skill of respecting personal space manifests in several ways:

Social Interaction Issues

Some students put their hands on other students or get too close in an attempt to engage others in a social interaction. In this situation, we teach consideration for others, issues of safety, appropriate attention-getting, and positive peer interactions.

Impulse Control Issues

Some students know (and want to respect) personal space, but they lack the restraint to do so. Younger children with typical ADHD hyperactivity traits will often put their hands on other students impulsively out of the sensory need to touch. Other students have emotional outbursts. They know they should not hit, but anger overtakes them and they reflexively cross the physical boundaries. In both instances, impulse control and practice is the best response.

Awareness Issues

Some students are simply not aware of how to navigate their body in space. They run into other individuals or knock items over as they pass. These students need direct teaching and specific strategies to bring awareness to this skill.

Interacting Positively with Peers and Adults/Being a Good Friend

This skill is the foundation for social interaction. For students, interactions can be student-to-peer or student-to-adult. Each of these types of interactions requires a different teaching method. Greetings, for example, are oftentimes different based on the person with whom you are speaking. We tend to use a more informal register with our friends. Students need to know how to navigate these differences.

There are many components to teaching positive interactions with others. I have always taught this skill by referencing three important behaviors:

1. Be inclusive.
2. Choose positive words.
3. Take thoughtful action.

This skill highlights one reason why unstructured play is such an important and needed activity in early childhood.

Play affords children the opportunity to learn how to interact with others. Unfortunately, more and more young people are in front of screens, and more screen time equals less face-to-face time. The more teachers at all levels integrate socialization into their teaching practices, the more practice our students will get learning this important skill.

Accepting Disappointment Appropriately/Conflict Resolution

In an earlier section, we discussed our society's focus on speed. We want what we want when we want it and we don't like to have to wait. Technology has conditioned us to expect instant gratification. Sadly, this is at odds with the reality that we don't always get what we want when we want it. Invariably, setbacks happen and conflicts with others occur. Students who understand the concept will be in a much better position to accept disappointments than those who do not.

Managing frustrations is one important subskill of accepting disappointment. For young children, we start by teaching them to use their words to express their feelings. As they get older, we teach skills of mindfulness and different ways to channel our feelings when things don't go the way we want.

Taking Responsibility for Our Actions

This skill takes time for mastery. When children are young, a natural reaction is to deny having done something in order to avoid getting in trouble. Though it is not the right way to handle the problem, it is a developmentally typical response. Of course, as we get older and learn ethical concepts of right and wrong, the goal is to take ownership of the choices we make.

PERSPECTIVE SHIFT

When behavior problems occur, educators sometimes miss out on opportunities to have students take responsibility for their actions. One way this happens is when we let students know we are calling their parents to report behavior issues. I encourage teachers and administrators to tell students, "When you go home tonight, talk to your parents about what happened in school today." By taking this approach, we are putting the ownership of the behavior in the student's hands to do so. This is one of the best ways to teach students how to take responsibility for their actions, while also reinforcing logical consequences. I still call the parents to give them a heads up, but I also ask the parents to allow their child the opportunity to own up to their behavior before addressing the issue. This gives the parents an opportunity to reinforce the good choice of taking ownership when appropriate, while also teaching alternative behaviors for any poor choices that were made.

Making Good Independent Choices

This foundational skill is the first step in being able to resist peer pressure. It is a difficult one for many students to master because of two opposing needs: the need to belong and the need to do the right thing. Because of our need to belong, it is difficult for some students to do the right thing when their friends are choosing to do something that is wrong. The skill of making good independent choices is rooted in ethical development which unfolds over a long period of time. As students get older, their ability to make independent choices naturally gets stronger. The hope, of course, is that the choices they choose to make are good ones.

Meet the Need. Teach the Skills.

Just as is the case with academics, students are at different levels of mastery with regard to these behavioral skills. Take the academic skill of reading, for example. Some students are more advanced in their reading development and are able to pick up the skill at a young age. However, others struggle, taking a great deal more time and development before the skill is mastered. Teachers expect these differences in academic development and differentiate support accordingly. The same should be true for supporting behavior. We should meet students where they are, with regard to behavioral instruction, and provide the support they need until skills are mastered.

Strategies for Behavioral Skill Development

If our goal is to strengthen students' abilities to work through the behavioral challenges they face, we need to implement strategies based on skill development. The following strategies will help us effectively meet this goal:

Identify Lifelong Behavioral Skills and Teach Them

There are specific behavior skills all students will need after they have left the school system. These skills should be communicated to the students and taught directly. For example, students at our school are taught they aren't always going to get what they want, so they need to be flexible. At the elementary level, we teach the students when they are told no by an adult to think to themselves, *Oh well, maybe next time*. Our hope is that by providing them with this strategy and practicing it in the school setting, they will be able to use it in other settings as well.

Use Lifelong Rationales Rather than Short-Term Consequences to Change Behavior

We want students to learn appropriate behaviors for a variety of settings. For this reason, we should emphasize natural and logical rationales for doing the right thing, rather than to avoid punishment.

- "When we treat others respectfully, we increase the chance they will do the same with us."
- "When we are quiet in the halls, we are being considerate of others."
- "When we use our time wisely, we have more time to do the things we want to do."

By connecting these skills to real-world application, we increase the chance they will be generalized in settings outside school.

Identify Gifts and Challenges and Set Goals

Once students know the behavioral skills expected, they should examine their own strengths and challenges, set goals, and routinely evaluate their progress:

Strength:

"Making friends is easy for me. I include others. I use kind words and take thoughtful actions."

Challenge:

"I have a very hard time controlling my anger. I want to use my words to express my feelings, but it's hard for me."

This process can be easily woven into different subjects by having students identify the character strengths and challenges of famous individuals across the curriculum. Additionally, students can integrate this into language arts through journaling and writing:

In your journal, write about one of Rosa Parks' challenges.

- She stood up for herself and didn't give in to peer pressure by sitting in the back of the bus.
- She showed perseverance and didn't give up when things got hard.

In the book in, *The Recess Queen,* what was one challenge for Mean Jean?

- She didn't respect the other students' personal space.
- She used hurtful words when talking to the other kids.

Provide Ongoing Feedback for Behavioral Progress and Setbacks

As students set behavioral goals, provide regular feedback on progress. Many teachers do this at report card or progress report time. Rather than evaluating the students, have them reflect on their own progress and provide feedback through coaching. A simple way to do this is to provide a set of skills and a rubric and have the students self-evaluate their progress. This type of activity provides great discussion and teaching opportunities.

SKILL	RATING
Following Directions	S
Paying Attention	A
Making Independent Good Choices	S

A – Always
M – Mostly
S – Sometimes
R – Rarely

This process teaches students to reflect on their behaviors, increasing the chance they will self-regulate in our absence.

Connect Consequences to Teachable Moments

The most important aspect of providing a consequence is providing students with teachable moments. When possible, use natural and logical consequences that help students make connections between their behavioral choices and the results of their actions. "When we use our time well during class, the classwork doesn't become homework," and "When we make a mess in a center, we clean it up before we get to transition to the next center."

CAUTION

"Assumicide" is the nemesis of this principle. All too often we assume students have mastered these behavioral skills and are just choosing not to use them. This is especially the case with regard to older students. Just because students are older physically doesn't mean they have the same behavioral skill set as their peers. This is why it is critical that the teaching of behavioral skills isn't confined to the elementary setting. We should be teaching important character education and life skills at all levels.

In Summary . . .

When a student struggles to understand an academic problem, we teach. If he or she doesn't master the skill, we re-teach. This process continues indefinitely until the skill is mastered and the student is successful. This should be the case with regard to behavior as well. When confronted with student misbehavior, the first question we need to ask is "What specific skill does this student need to master?" If students shout out in class, they need help internalizing the skill of getting attention appropriately. If students argue when corrected, they need to be taught how to accept criticism. This principle requires educators to shift their perspective about the best ways to create

> *When confronted with student misbehavior, the first question we need to ask is "What specific skill does this student need to master?"*

long-term behavior change. Ultimately, behavior is better improved through education than punishment.

FINAL THOUGHT

When problems arise, educators should focus on creating teachable moments to shape behaviors. As skills are developed, the likelihood that positive behaviors will strengthen will increase.

Crisis Principles

Students who exhibit chronic behavior problems need the highest level of support. The last two principles build on the first seven and require us to make a shift in both our perspective and strategies. By understanding basic principles about stress, behavioral patterns, and the brain, we can avoid our natural inclination of pitfalls and become better able to respond in a way that strengthens positive behaviors. These two principles have strong implications for working not only with our students, but also colleagues, parents, and family members alike.

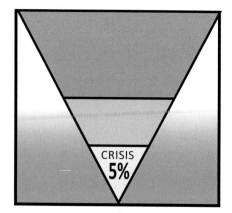

8. When overly stressed, the thinking brain **shuts down**.

   We all deal with a certain amount of stress in our daily lives; however, when eustress (good, normal amounts of stress) becomes distress (bad, high levels of stress), the rational thinking parts of our brain defer to the irrational survival structures. The stressed brain icon provides a visual cue for identifying and supporting individuals in a state of crisis.

9. Behaviors are often the result of **ingrained habits.**

When the same pathways in the brain are used repeatedly, they become worn. For students with continual behavior concerns, there is a strong chance these repeated patterns move from a place of conscious choice to reflexive habits. The road icon serves to remind us of this point. By understanding the nature of habits, we can work to help our students develop positive behavioral patterns and break those of concern.

PRINCIPLE
EIGHT

When Overly Stressed, the Thinking Brain Shuts Down

Puberty. It's amazing we all make it through the teen years. Hormones can wreak havoc on otherwise normally functioning individuals, and unfortunately middle and high school teachers get a front-row seat to watch how things play out. Working at all levels, I'm often asked the question, "Do you find high school or early childhood to be the most challenging when it comes to dealing with behaviors?" My response is always the same: "Neither. It's middle school." Neurologically, I believe students at this level get hijacked by their emotions regularly, which can lead to mood swings and, invariably, power struggles.

Poor Timing, to Say the Least

As I recall, spring break was on the horizon. Teachers were on edge, students were on edge, and the administrators were trying to juggle the needs of everyone and just keep the wheels on the bus. Unfortunately, behavior concerns were a huge issue for this school. I received a call from the vice principal around 9:00 a.m. requesting my help. As a behavior consultant at our regional service center, calls like this were not unusual, especially around this time of year.

By the time I arrived at the school, there was a line of students in the office, all holding discipline referrals, waiting to be seen by an administrator. The vice principal met me just as I walked into the office. "I'm glad you are here. Thoughts?" he asked me, as he pointed to all the students. "Teachers keep sending them. This is what we deal with every day!" There was an awkward silence as the students, school secretary, and vice principal looked at me, waiting for a response. "Let's go into your office," I replied.

I shut the door to the administrator's office to give him a chance to calm down. He was clearly overwhelmed and frustrated. However, before we had a chance to sit down, the secretary popped her head in. "Sorry to bother you, sir, but I have Paul and Adrian out here. Coach had to pull them apart. They were fighting again." I followed the administrator back into the main office and saw the two boys when we rounded the corner. They were still visibly upset, and I was certain if the coach had not been standing between them, they would have continued the fight.

"Really, Paul?" the vice principal said, clearly annoyed. "What did I tell you would happen if you showed up at my office again for fighting?" It was obvious the student was taken aback by these words, as well as by the tone and volume with which they were said. His reaction was swift. "You can't call my pops! He'll kill me!" he said very loudly, simultaneously picking up the edge of the nearby desk and flipping it over. The secretary jumped back just before the desk landed on her foot. At this point, the coach intervened and had to restrain the student before escorting him to the cool-down room. A few days later I learned Paul was referred to the alternative school for this offense.

It wasn't until after spring break that I returned to the school, and by that time things had settled down. The administrator asked me for suggestions, so together we mapped out the last portion of the incident:

- The student was very upset and in a state of crisis.
- The administrator referenced the consequence of the father being called.
- The student flipped the desk.

I asked the administrator why he mentioned the consequence of the call home when the student was that upset. "I wanted him to know that fighting is unacceptable," he answered. The problem, of course, is one of timing. When individuals are in a crisis state, they are not open to feedback. Mentioning the consequence at that time triggered the reaction of the desk getting flipped. This doesn't excuse the student's behavior, but the situation would have probably played out differently if the consequences had been discussed at a later time.

Brain Science 101

When designing supports for severe behaviors, it is important to have a basic understanding of the human brain. In his book *The Triune Brain in Evolution*, neuroscientist Dr. Paul MacLean formulated a model dividing the brain into three smaller brain regions of anatomy and function. The book was released in the 1960s and, although the model has been criticized as being oversimplified and been revised given new discoveries about the brain, core ideas still have strong behavioral implications.[18]

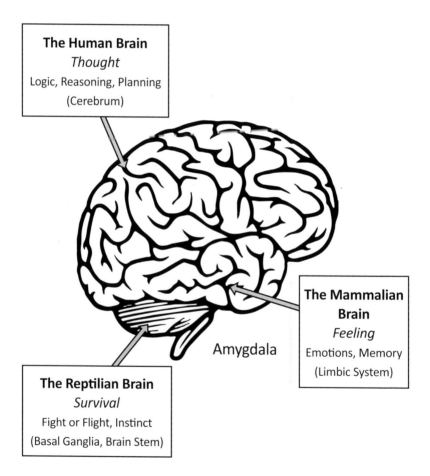

The Human Brain
Thought
Logic, Reasoning, Planning
(Cerebrum)

The Mammalian Brain
Feeling
Emotions, Memory
(Limbic System)

Amygdala

The Reptilian Brain
Survival
Fight or Flight, Instinct
(Basal Ganglia, Brain Stem)

The upper part of the brain houses the cerebrum and structures responsible for thought, inclusive of logic, reasoning, and planning. The mid regions of the brain house the limbic system, key areas responsible for emotions and memory. The lower regions house the basal ganglia, brain stem, and other structures responsible for survival.

One critical structure in the mid-brain area is called the amygdala. The amygdala are two clusters of nuclei in the limbic system which act as an affective filter. When information enters the brain, the amygdala processes the emotional content. If negative emotions are triggered, including fear or anxiety, key areas in the lower brain regions are activated. When the associations are positive, information is more likely to be processed in the upper regions of the brain.

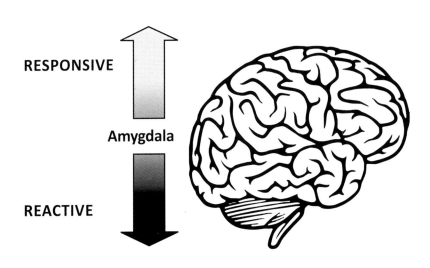

RESPONSIVE

Amygdala

REACTIVE

The Responsive Brain

Ever had a really great day at school? Let's set the scene. You wake up rested, eat breakfast, experience little to no traffic, and get to school early. The students enter your room quietly and follow your directions. All lessons go according to plan and you have very few disruptions. After lunch you get an unscheduled short observation from your administrator, and it goes very well. On your way out the door at the end of the day, you stop by your box and find a positive note from your administrator about the walk-through. As you leave the building and enter the parking lot, one of your colleagues stops her car, signaling you to go first before she proceeds. You respond with a smile and wave, and tell her to have a great weekend. Life is good.

The Reactive Brain

Now, let's switch things up. Ever had a really bad day at school? You wake up late, have no time to grab a bite to eat or coffee, and get stuck in traffic, causing you to be late for work. The students enter your room completely out of control and don't appear to have any interest in following your directions. You discover you left your lesson plan book at home, so you have to wing it. Your lunch is cut short because of an unscheduled parent visit, so you return to class in a very unpleasant mood. Your classroom is locked so your students are waiting outside the door when you arrive. You notice your administrator is also waiting to enter for a short unscheduled observation. You are not pleased with the observation but are glad when your administrator leaves. Relieved the day is finally over, you stop by your box in the office and find a note about your observation, which did not go well at all. You walk outside to discover it is pouring down rain. Just as you step into the parking lot, you come to an abrupt stop as one of your colleagues darts out of her parking spot, almost hits you, and drenches you with water in the process. Do you wave to her in thanks and tell her to have a great weekend? Or is your reaction something much less polite? Life is not good.

We all have great social skills when we don't need to use them. When things are going well, we are able to think, stay calm, use our words, and understand cause and effect.

> *We all have great social skills when we don't need to use them.*

However, when threat is perceived, the lower survival regions of our brain take over. We tend to be irrational, have tunnel vision, and are driven by our emotional state. During these times, we react and behave impulsively. When overly stressed, the upper thinking regions of the brain tend to shut down and the lower regions take over. This is especially the case for students with chronic behavioral problems.

"I'm Not Ready" and "I'm Not Listening"

Students with chronic behavior problems are in continual states of reacting rather than responding. This creates problems because you can't teach new behaviors to a person who is in survival mode. When overly stressed, our *input* is turned off and our *output* is turned on. The more anxious and upset we are, the less open we are to receiving feedback about our behavior at that time. So when we intervene is as important as how we intervene. If we try to engage students in rational conversations while they are overly stressed, power struggles are likely to ensue.

Power Struggles: Control and Aggression

As discussed in an earlier chapter, we have the need for a sense of control. When we are in control, we feel safe. Unfortunately, for many students, there are many factors, both external and internal, over which they have little control:

- Divorced Parents
- Poor Social Skills
- Anger Issues
- Academic Concerns
- Home Issues (dad incarcerated, older sibling in the hospital, death of a grandparent)

The more we experience a lack of control in one area of our life, the more likely we are to try to gain control in other areas to compensate. In the classroom, power struggles are often the result of students and teachers competing for control. The student is trying to regain some sense of control while the teacher is working to not lose control of the situation and class.

. . . power struggles are often the result of students and teachers competing for control.

Additionally, when we move into states of crisis, a natural reaction is to become aggressive. At a basic survival level, when someone pushes us, our reactive inclination is to push back. This instinct only exacerbates tenuous situations with students. As we get older, we learn how to channel and inhibit our aggressive instincts, but our students have had less time to develop these skills. So, it is not uncommon to see both verbal and physical aggression tendencies from students who have more severe behavior concerns.

De-Escalation Strategies

The implications of this one principle are great. If our goal is to stay out of power struggles with students and help them manage their behavior in productive ways, we must apply the information about the responsive and reactive regions of the brain to daily practice. The following strategies help us do this:

Model Expected Behaviors

As highlighted earlier, modeled behaviors are internalized. Since emotions are prioritized over words, feedback is provided to a person in crisis through tone and volume of voice, rate of speech, and other non-verbal cues such as body language and facial expressions. Emotions feed emotions, so when we interact with people who are very emotional, our emotional states are altered.[19] When a student is in a crisis state, calm emotions from others are needed. The more we are able to provide neutral emotional feedback to students in crisis, the less likely we will be to potentially feed their crisis states.

Think About It . . .

Are there individuals in your life who calm you down and ground you when you are in an emotional tailspin? Are there others who, due to their heightened emotional state, inadvertently escalate things? When we are upset, it is best to surround ourselves with people who quell the turbulence. Our students need the same.

Ignore Words

Individuals often say things they don't mean when they are angry. The words are coming from their heightened emotional state and are used to convey their emotions. When a young child shouts, "I hate you!" they rarely mean it. They're the words that reflexively pop out when a child is having a difficult time accepting disappointment. In essence, they are saying, "I'm angry, but I can't find the right words to articulate why." This is especially the case for younger students. As they get older, however, the hope is that, through instruction and healthy modeling, they learn to inhibit these comments and manage their emotions appropriately.

When students say inappropriate comments, rather than responding to the comment at that time, reflect back the feelings. You can always address specific words and teach alternatives at a later time.

Student: I hate this class.
Teacher: You're upset.

Student: This is stupid.
Teacher: Sometimes work can be frustrating.

This technique sends the message, "I hear you. I know you are angry." It also directly models for our students the words we want them to use when managing their feelings in the future.

PERSPECTIVE *SHIFT*

After a student conflict, adults' first inclination is usually to establish the facts of the situation. "What happened?" we ask students. The problem with this question is one of timing. When individuals are in an escalated emotional state, the rational thought process is disrupted, therefore the details they recount are based on feelings more so than facts. I once asked a teenager to tell me what happened after an incident. "James hit me!" he said. However, once the student calmed down, he reconsidered: "Well . . . he didn't really hit me, but he was going to." Students should always be in a de-escalated state prior to discussing problems and teaching alternative behaviors.

Step Away and Watch Timing

Have you ever had someone tell you what you did wrong when you were upset? How receptive were you to that information? Engaging students and trying to have a rational discussion when they're very upset will most likely lead to power struggles. When students are at risk for hurting self or others, adults must intervene. However, trying to teach or issue consequences when students are in crisis situations will, most likely, not yield the best results. Allow time and space to quell turbulent emotions. A person can't remain in crisis indefinitely. If a student is refusing to follow directions or continually trying to engage you, say, "You're upset. I get upset too. We can talk about this later." This allows the student time to regain composure before debriefing the situation.

Use Distraction to Shift the Focus

When in a crisis state the brain tends to hyperfocus. When we feel as though we were wronged, it is very hard for the amygdala to "let things go." We play the event over and over in our head, emotionally spinning in circles. It is not until we are distracted in some way that we are able to effectively come out of our escalated emotional state and calm down. Distraction is a great strategy for moving past a crisis. Here are some simple strategies for shifting the attention:

- Reference a non-school related activity: "I saw you at the game last night."
- Comment on clothing: "Are those new shoes?"

- Avert eye contact and use self-talk: "I need to clean up this mess on my desk."
- Give the student a task: "Can you do me a favor and put these over there?"

The idea is to draw attention away from the behavioral trigger of the crisis.

Remove the Audience (or Yourself)

Since attention magnifies behavior, the more individuals around during a crisis state, the more potential there is for that crisis to escalate. We should work to remove any audience of students, as this will allow the person in crisis to work through things without being triggered back into crisis by others. At times, I have removed myself from a situation by telling a student, "I want to give you my undivided attention and hear what happened, so let me take care of this first." I then walk out of the room for a minute. This keeps me from inadvertently escalating the student. It is also a great distraction tool.

Get Physical

Physical activity is a very important strategy for de-escalation. When students are sitting still in crisis, neurologically, the brain locks down to some degree. However, when a student is moving, more oxygen is released, blood flow is better, and chemicals are released to reestablish homeostasis and move beyond the survival state. This does not mean students have to do aerobic exercises. The strategy can be as simple as asking a student to take a note to a teacher. Many administrators will simply say, "Walk with me for a minute." Not only does the strategy prime the brain for de-escalation physically, but cognitively, the movement usually serves as another distraction, which helps as well.

Provide Feedback after the Crisis Is Over

Behavior is strengthened through skill development, which means our ultimate goal is to teach replacement behaviors. This is best accomplished when a person is in a rational state. When a student calms down, cycle back around and work through the conflict. "Pat, you were really angry when we got back from gym. Let's talk about what happened." This is the time to validate feelings: "It's okay to get upset." This is also the time to teach replacement behaviors: "Let's talk about how we can handle things differently next time."

Teach Self-Regulation Strategies

The best way to help students cope with crisis situations is to help them identify self-soothing strategies: "Shannon, when you are upset or angry, what do you do that helps you calm down?" Teaching emotional management strategies—counting to ten, taking deep breaths, centering exercises, and other methods of mindfulness—helps students self-regulate their behaviors. This is our ultimate goal: to help students help themselves rather than being dependent on us for this type of emotional support.

Work as a Team

When trying to support crisis behaviors, work with your colleagues. Since behaviors mainly occur in a relationship, you must alter the relationship in order to alter the behavior. Sometimes, one teacher can say something to a student that causes behaviors to escalate, but another teacher can say the same thing and get a completely different response from the student. By working as a team we can discover which relationships yield better results and make choices about interventions accordingly.

By working as a team we can discover which relationships yield better results and make choices about interventions accordingly.

Parent Strategies

The strategies above are designed to support individuals in crisis behaviors, so they can be implemented with more than just our students. They can be especially helpful in working with the parents of our students as well. When working with parents, consider the following:

- Listen more than talk. Allow parents the opportunity to provide their input. I often tell parents, "You know your son better than I ever will. Please tell me what I can do differently to help him." This goes a long way in validating the opinions of your parents while also strengthening your relationship with them in the process.

- When a parent sends an email with an angry overtone, respond with a call or face-to-face meeting. Emotions cloud the written word and email responses will most likely be misinterpreted. In these situations, parents most often become defensive.

- Don't tell parents about what their children are doing wrong when they approach you in an angry state. Allow them to vent and give them feedback about their child at a later time.

- Parents, like students, naturally have stronger relationships with some individuals than others. Seek out the staff members who have the best relationship with the parents, as they will be the ones best equipped to de-escalate them when they are overly stressed.

CAUTION

One of the most important steps in dealing with crisis behaviors occurs after the crisis is over. Once calm, it is critical to discuss the incident and teach alternative prosocial behaviors. A teacher once said to me, "Jason's calm. And happy. Why would I want to poke the sleeping bear and awaken the inner beast? He will just fly off the handle. Things are better. We don't need to revisit them." The problem with this line of reasoning is that by not providing a teachable moment, the student is not afforded an opportunity to learn from his mistakes. Additionally, by not putting closure on an incident, we increase the likelihood the crisis will habitually occur again.

In Summary . . .

Reactions or responses can escalate or de-escalate, accordingly. When calm, individuals can be rational, understand cause and effect, make good decisions, and think clearly. When overly stressed, impulsive, emotional, and reactionary behaviors surface. It is important to understand this concept because it is the foundation for dealing with difficult behaviors. When people are very angry or overly stressed, they are not receptive to feedback. If our goal is to strengthen positive behaviors, we must understand that when we intervene is just as important as how we intervene. By not engaging individuals during periods of distress, adults are better able to defuse potential power struggles and, ultimately, better model calm behaviors at a more emotionally neutral time.

FINAL THOUGHT

When an individual is in crisis, the first job is to de-escalate. Once calm and rational, discussions can be had, and new behaviors can be taught.

PRINCIPLE
NINE

Behaviors Are Often the Result of Ingrained Habits

Mind Your Manners

Having been raised a South Louisiana Cajun boy, I'm most definitely a product of my environment. My momma raised me in a way that exudes my heritage from every pore of my being. I wasn't really aware of how much so until I moved to Chicago for graduate school. I was at a drive-through window ordering some food after having just arrived in my new city. The voice from the speaker asked, "What can I get you?" I answered, "I'll have a number three, please." "Would you like the meal deal?" she continued. "Yes ma'am," I instinctively replied, at which point, there was no reply, just a long period of silence. I waited to be asked to drive up to the window, but instead I heard, "You're not from around here, are you?" Of course, my final reply confirmed her suspicion. "No ma'am. I'm not."

Soon after, I realized these two phrases, specifically "Yes ma'am/sir" and "No ma'am/sir," which came so naturally to me, were off-putting to some individuals. In trying to be sensitive to the needs of others, I worked to adjust my answers and respond with just yes and no. I quickly discovered how difficult it would be to make that change. It wasn't until I replaced ma'am/sir with other words, like "Yes, please" and "No, thank you," that I was able to comfortably change my habitual speech patterns.

Not long after graduate school I returned to the south and reverted back to using my "Yes ma'am" manners in the way my momma intended. I also tried to pass on the use of good manners to my children. When they were young, I was rather insistent on them using words like *please, thank you, you're welcome, excuse me*. Every time the opportunity arose, I prompted the boys to use these phrases so they would get into the habit of doing so. And they did well when they were young. However, as they moved into their teen years, it seemed they had forgotten everything their mother and I taught them. I felt as though I was constantly reminding them to use basic manners when talking with us.

It wasn't until we moved my second-born son to college that I was able to see the positive results of our efforts. I remember being so surprised at hearing my son use all the phrases associated with good manners in almost every interaction he had. "Whoa!" I said. "Where is this coming from? You really do use good manners when you are not at home." His reply helped me understand the nature of habits and how they can be shaped. "Dad, I've never really thought about it, but I always use good manners with people outside our family. I'm just not in the habit of using them with you because you're my dad. That would be weird."

Creatures of Habit

When someone mentions the word *habit*, individuals immediately think of specific traditional examples—nail biting, cursing, thumb sucking, leg shaking, or, in my wife's case, breaking a sugar addiction. However, rarely do you hear the term used when describing student behaviors. I believe this is due to our assumption that poor behaviors are most often the result of poor choices. The more I learn about the brain and the older I get, the more convinced I am of the flaw in this line of reasoning.

The human brain is an amazing organ. It takes in an infinite amount of information through our senses, yet it can only consciously attend to one thing at a time. What does it attend to? Whatever is most important. In order to focus on what is most important, repeated tasks are often relegated to automation. Accordingly, the brain is constantly looking for patterns in the environment. When a pattern is detected, a mental notation is filed away in the hippocampus, parallel structures in our brain that are critical for memory formation and retention. Each time the pattern is repeated, the memory is strengthened. The more this happens, the more the task becomes automated, and thus, the less the brain has to consciously attend to it. This frees the brain up to attend to more important tasks crucial to our survival.

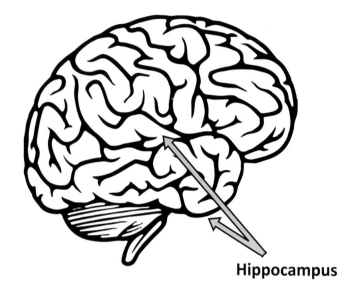

Hippocampus

Examples of this process play out in schools daily. On the first day of school when routines are new, teachers spend a great deal of time teaching and focusing students' attention on expectations. The novelty of the information heightens attention levels in the class. However, each day as the routines are reviewed, the less students must actively attend in order to carry them out. After a few weeks, the majority of students are carrying out the routines out of habit. This is the process by which tasks move from a state of novelty to a state of ritual.

Think About It . . .

It's not just classroom routines that get filed away into a habitual state. Teachers know that after the first few weeks of school, the attention spans of students often wander. This is because when tasks are first introduced, the brain is on high alert. However, if the pattern of instruction is repeated too systematically, the novelty wears off, tasks become automated, and attention levels drop—Come class . . . open up the computer . . . listen to the lecture . . . take notes. Many students can habitually do this routine and still consciously focus on other tasks, like texting or talking to a friend or doing other assignments. This is why effective teaching should incorporate a balance of both ritual and novelty.

Auto-Drive

Habits are established with repeated behaviors. For many years, I had a similar morning routine. I woke up, let our dogs out, took a shower, made a protein shake, and headed off to school. I never really thought about this pattern until I couldn't remember having gone through it. I can't tell you the number of mornings I got to school, looked down at my hand and saw my shake, only to think, *I don't remember making this shake! What did I put in it?* or thinking, *Did I let the dog out this morning? I can't remember.* A danger of repeated behaviors is that they become automatic, unconscious, less about choice and more about habits. This does not mean that students don't make poor choices. We all make poor choices at times; however, the more students get into patterns of misbehavior, the more apt those behaviors are to develop into poor habits.

Strongly Ingrained Patterns

In looking at behaviors on the PBS triangle, the 80 percent of students who respond to prevention efforts are likely to have infrequent misbehavior. Because of this, their misbehavior is less likely to be a result of habit, and potentially more so about choice. However, when students begin to drop into the categories of needing intervention and crisis levels of support, the greater the chance the behaviors become ingrained patterns or habits. As with any behavior, the more frequent the occurance, the stronger the habitual patterns become.[20] Again, this is not to imply that students in crisis never make bad choices, but to assume all behaviors are the result of poor choice is problematic for many reasons.

> . . . to assume all behaviors are the result of poor choice is problematic for many reasons.

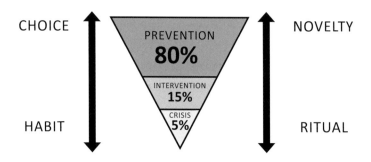

Behavioral Compounded Interest

When students first enter school in the primary grades, teachers are patient with them because they understand it takes time to learn behavioral expectations. Teachers' tolerance levels are generally higher with younger children, so when they misbehave, teachers assume positive intent:

- *He's never been to school before.*
- *She's young for her age.*
- *He's not had a lot of interaction with other children.*
- *He doesn't know better yet.*
- *He hasn't learned how to behave.*

As children get older, however, behavioral expectations change. With maturity, we expect students to make better choices, and we often assume misbehavior is the result of poor choices. As discussed earlier, the problem with this line of reasoning is that there are a variety of other reasons for poor behavior, and if we don't acknowledge the reasons, the problems begin to build upon each other.

Think of this as a problem of *behavioral compounded interest*. A student might start out with a mild behavior problem due to young development. If this issue is not acknowledged and supported, frustration sets in, which triggers additional problems. The problem is now compounded, and additional incidents continue the cycle, increasing the likelihood for strong poor behavioral habits and thought patterns to form.

Fast-forward to high school where some students have experienced years of behavioral failure.

Is it any wonder why many of these students give up? Unfortunately, the age at which children are giving up is getting younger each year. Several decades ago, apathy and frustration due to misbehavior was seen in high school. Then we started seeing this phenomenon with middle school students. Unfortunately, we are now seeing this pattern of apathy and resignation in students even younger. This mindset of resignation is understandable when we look at the roll habits play in the shaping of behavior.

 **PERSPECTIVE** *SHIFT*

Have you ever tried to lose weight? Exercise more? Stop chewing your nails? Chances are good you might have given up before you found success When we don't feel as though we can succeed, giving up becomes an appealing choice. Students are no different.

- *"Why should I try? I'm just going to get in trouble anyway."*
- *"Just send me to the office. That's what you're going to do eventually."*
- *"I don't care."*

Do any of these phrases sound familiar? Each one represents a student who is giving up and losing hope. It is very common for students with poor behavioral habits to give up. They get overwhelmed from continual failure to change the behavior and stop trying, which is what we, as adults, often do.

I Give Up

Breaking habits is very difficult. We know it will be hard. We expect to have intermittent failures along the way. And for most of us, we are more likely to stop trying than to persist and find success. Our students are no different. They often simply give up out of frustration. And if this happens and our students stop putting forth effort, our interventions will never succeed. Additionally, the negative cycle of trying and failing eventually damages self-esteem, which over the long-haul is a much bigger problem than the misbehavior itself.

We Are in This Together

The good news is that since behavior mainly occurs in a relationship, as adults, we can help students break their poor habits by changing our interactions with them. Unfortunately, the opposite is true as well. When students draw adults into power struggles repeatedly, each power struggle serves to further ingrain the habit of fighting as a way of working through problems. For example, when an adult repeatedly sends a student to the office, the misbehavior and referral becomes an interactional habit. Sadly, this habit can teach the student to give up when conflict occurs. The cycle can also serve to lower the student's self-esteem. However, if we work through the problem in the classroom, we can change the habit in a positive way. By doing so, we not only teach the student the important lesson of healthy conflict resolution, but we also teach them ways to persist and work through our differences. As an added bonus, the healthy resolution of the problem can also serve to raise a student's self-esteem.

Counselors Needed

It's not just outward behaviors we are trying to change. A student's self-perception and self-esteem can be damaged when repeated failure is the result of their efforts. This is why it is critical that counselors and other mental health professionals be present in the school system. Students with chronic behavior problems will benefit more from time with these individuals than any amount of time spent in detention or time out.

Behavioral Code-Switching

Students learn different skills for different settings, so no matter how deeply patterns are ingrained in one setting, the patterns can be changed in a different setting. Environmental cues help the brain compartmentalize survival efforts. We've all seen students behave very differently around their parents than they do with us. As educators, we think to ourselves, *I can't believe Alex is talking to his mother that way. He would never do that with me!* This is a good example of behavioral code-switching, where a student learns a different interactional pattern based on repeated behaviors in one setting. This does not mean the child is necessarily being manipulative; he has just developed a different habit of interactions with his mother in the home setting.

Hope for Change

This ability of students to code-switch should give educators hope for changing the ingrained behavioral patterns of their students. However, for change to occur, educators must move away from assuming poor behaviors are merely the result of poor choices. If we continue to respond to behavioral habits as choices, we will further ingrain the very behaviors we are trying to extinguish in our students. We must understand that changing habits requires a different set of strategies than simply issuing traditional consequences.

Strategies for Reshaping Ingrained Habits

Habits are like roadways in the brain. The more they are used, the stronger the pathways get. Retraining unhealthy ingrained patterns in the brain takes time, but it can be done. Try applying these strategies to shape healthy behavioral patterns in your students.

Start with Yourself

Changing a habit is hard for students and even harder for adults because the older we are, the longer we've had to create and solidify our habits. And, again, since behavior mainly occurs in a relationship, the first step in altering the habits of our students is examining our own habits of interaction with them, meaning we must start with ourselves. If we don't change our behaviors that lead to power struggles with students, we make it more challenging for them to break their own habits in the process. By altering our responses, body language, and when and how we provide attention, we disrupt the existing habits and allow new, healthier ones to develop.

Assume Positive Intent

Approach behavior change and habit-breaking from the perspective that we all do the best we are able given the

> *Approach behavior change and habit-breaking from the perspective that we all do the best we are able given the skills at our disposal.*

skills at our disposal. Habits are habits for a reason—they are unconscious reactions rather than choices. This does not excuse poor behavior, but understanding this concept helps us design the best strategies for reshaping behavior in a positive way. Assuming positive intent also gets adults into the habit of choosing a path of empathy and understanding rather than one of judgment.

Teach Students About Habits

Traditional punishments rely on "doing to" strategies— calling home, sending students to the office, etc. These strategies rely on outside control and external means for behavior change. Rather, use a "working with" approach. Teach students about the nature and language of habits. Help them understand how habits develop and ways to break unhealthy ones. When we do this, we provide students with a healthy way to understand their behaviors and increase their ability to self-regulate in our absence.

Teaching students about their habits also indirectly reinforces the concept of separating the behavior from the student. Just because a student makes a poor choice or gets into a bad habit does not mean she is a bad person.

Our goal is to help students change their behaviors and habits while keeping their healthy self-esteem intact.

Strengthen Awareness by Focusing Attention

Attention is a powerful tool in breaking habits. Just as distraction can be used to interrupt power struggles, so too can focus be used in breaking habits. Drawing attention to a pattern helps a person become more aware, and awareness leads to choice. When we teach our students to recognize their habits, we are empowering them to make choices to change them.

Strengthen awareness by continuously referring to the language of habits in your daily interactions with students.

- "Remember, the more that happens, the more likely it will turn into a habit, and poor habits are hard to break."
- "You've gotten into a great habit of sitting in a spot in class that helps you make good choices, Quinton."
- "Denise, let's talk about the habit we have gotten into when you don't turn in your work. I'm wondering how you and I can change our interaction when that happens."

Keeping the focus on habits is also a great way to decrease the likelihood students get defensive when confronted about behavior. Directing the discussion toward habits is less confrontational than discussing behaviors directly.

Practice for Automation

Just as behaviors are strengthened through skill development, so too are patterns strengthened through practice. Help students break poor habits by practicing replacement behaviors until the new ones become automated. Examples of ways to practice can include:

- Following a set of directions
- Paying attention while a passage is being read
- Walking in the halls rather than running
- Using appropriate language to work through a conflict with another student

Practicing skills not only increases the chance that new habits are formed, but it also helps students learn new healthier behavior skills in the process. When students complain about having to practice, remind them, "The more we practice, the better we get. Practice helps us develop better habits."

As anyone who has tried to exercise more or swear less can attest, breaking a habit is hard business. Our ultimate goal is for students to leave the school system with the academic and behavioral tools they need to be successful. This goal is not accomplished in one year. Similarly, it is not realistic for students who have ingrained patterns of behavior to be able to change those habits quickly. Change takes time. Concentrating on incremental progress rather than the end result of

CAUTION

what we are trying to achieve accomplishes several things:

- It lessens frustration levels (for us and our students).
- It helps our students see change as possible.
- It helps us celebrate small victories.
- It strengthens positive relationships with our students.

As the disturbing adage goes, "How do you eat an elephant? One bite at a time." Focusing on the process of change gives us all the permission to be more patient and understanding with our students, which is ultimately the best way to accomplish our long-term goal of positive behavior change.

In Summary . . .

Students who demonstrate repeated behavior concerns tend to develop deeply ingrained habits. Changing these behaviors can be very challenging. When students demonstrate inappropriate behaviors, a teacher's response or reaction will often either strengthen the pattern or disrupt it. The most effective teachers are able to minimize attention to these behaviors while using other techniques, such as distraction, to extinguish them. The ultimate goal of our interventions is to lessen the amount of time the student exhibits these behaviors so new habits can be formed. Long-term, lasting behavior change is a process. If a student has had many years of behavior patterning, reshaping the habits will take time. The good news is that students can effectively create different patterns based on environmental cues. A student could function on very unhealthy patterns at home, while still having healthy interactions at school. The patterns are shaped by our daily responses or reactions, accordingly.

FINAL THOUGHT

When students exhibit repeated inappropriate behaviors, adults should work to disrupt these patterns quickly in an attempt to shape healthy, more appropriate ones.

Positive Behavior Principles
THE BIG PICTURE

A Lot to Take in

"My brain hurts," a teacher once told me after attending staff development on the Positive Behavior Principles. "It's great stuff, but I'm going to need some time to decide where to start."

I get it. When taking in new information, it can feel overwhelming. It's not simply a matter of reading the book and trying all the strategies. Just as it takes time for students to change their behaviors, it takes time for us to digest information and put new strategies into practice.

I regularly present the principles at schools on professional development days. The response seems to be the same. The information is always well-received, but I wonder how much change will take place on the campus as a result of the work. I let participants know that my presentation can't accurately be assessed at the end of the day. An evaluation at that time only lets administrators know if participants enjoyed the day. My evaluation comes weeks afterward based on whether or not the information is implemented, which is a process that takes time.

One way to think about the process of integrating new information into practice is by examining the memory systems of the brain. When you are first reading this book, the information is processed by immediate memory. Think of immediate memory as a clipboard, on which you place the content. The information that does not resonate might be dropped off the clipboard and out of immediate memory, but important and salient points are moved from immediate to working memory. Think of working memory as a desk. You put information on the desk while organizing it, deciding what you will keep and what you will discard. If you think you will use the information, it is moved to short-term memory. Think of short-term memory as a series of file folders where you store the information while trying it out. If you find success with the information, you take all the file folders and put them in a file cabinet for safe keeping. This file cabinet represents long-term memory.

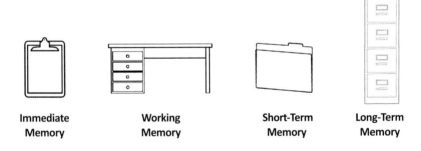

| Immediate Memory | Working Memory | Short-Term Memory | Long-Term Memory |

This model is based on the work of Dr. David Sousa in his book, *How the Brain Learns*.[21] As illustrated, this model highlights how the flow of information moves from one memory system to the next. This transfer doesn't happen overnight. It is an incremental process.

I believe that educators best create long-term behavior change in students when we slowly shift our perspectives and simultaneously adapt our strategies accordingly. This happens in very small steps, but over time the cumulative effect can be powerful. It is better to move through the integration process of the principles, as noted above, slowly and purposefully rather than trying to digest and implement all of them at once.

Complementary Practices

In isolation, each of the nine principles is powerful. They help us see behaviors differently and, as a result, adjust our strategies in a positive way. However, collectively, the principles can be transformational. Because they are complementary, many of the principles build on the others:

- By infusing more movement and talk time throughout our lessons (principle 3), we infuse more novelty, breaking up instruction and increasing engagement (principle 2).

- By better understanding our students' developmental levels (principle 6), we are better able to target specific behavioral skills and teach them (principle 7).

- By drawing attention away from misbehavior (principle 5), we have the opportunity to shift our focus and channel students' behaviors by giving them active tasks when they are making good choices (principle 3).

- By modeling appropriate behaviors (principle 4) when overly stressed, we are better able to stay out of power struggles with students (principle 8).

- By working with students repeatedly to practice deficit social skills (principle 7), students are more likely to be successful in breaking their poor behavioral habits and developing positive new ones (principle 9).

- By not engaging students in power struggles (principle 8), we gain students' trust, which strengthens our relationships with them (principle 1).

As discussed at the onset of the book, behaviors do not occur in isolation. Our behaviors are based on our belief system. Just as the principles complement each other, so too must our beliefs and practices. One of the best ways to find success with the nine principles is by adjusting our perspective and focusing on the bigger picture of what we are trying to accomplish.

Character Development

Although this body of work focuses on how to strengthen student behaviors, we also need to keep in mind the reasons why we should do so. Our behaviors are an indication of our character. Positive behavior is a short-term goal, but healthy character is the endgame. We want our students to grow up to be good people, not just simply well-behaved ones. We want them to be ethical—making good choices because they have an internal compass helping them to do so, rather than simply behaving to avoid punishments or gain rewards. We also hope they are able to look outside their own needs and develop a sense of compassion, understanding, and concern for others.

> *Positive behavior is a short-term goal, but healthy character is the endgame.*

These are the long-term goals. Keeping our focus on character development helps us shift our perspective, ultimately moving away from strategies encouraging short-term compliance to ones that foster long-term healthy behavioral change.

POSITIVE Behavior Principles

PREVENTION

Behavior mainly occurs in a **relationship**

Effective teaching incorporates a balance of **ritual** and **novelty**

 It is easier to **channel** behavior than to stop it

Modeled behaviors are internalized

INTERVENTION

 Attention magnifies behavior

Developmental levels influence behaviors

 Positive behaviors are strengthened through **skill development**

CRISIS

When overly stressed, the thinking brain **shuts down**

 Behaviors are often the result of ingrained **habits**

Notes

[1] "Positive Behavioral Interventions and Support: Brief Introduction." Center on PBIS, June 29, 2018, https://assets-global.website-files. com/5d3725188825e071f1670246/5d7bd792f6de3210d90755a6_what%20is%20 pbis%20q%26a%2030%20june%202018.pdf.

[2] Rhitu Chatterjee, "School Shooters: What's Their Path To Violence?" NPR, February 10, 2019, https://www.npr.org/sections/health-shots/2019/02/10/690372199/school-shooters-whats-their-path-to-violence.

[3] Brad Bushman, Patrick E. Jamieson, Ilana Weitz, and Daniel Romer, "Gun Violence Trends in Movies," Pediatrics: *Official Journal of the American Academy of Pediatrics*, December 2013, 132 (6) 1014-1018, https://doi.org/10.1542/ peds.2013-1600.

[4] Patricia Scully and Jacqueline Howell, "Using Rituals and Traditions to Create Classroom Community for Children, Teachers, and Parents," *Early Childhood Education Journal*, Volume 36 (3): October 4, 2008.

[5] David A. Sousa, *How the Brain Learns* (Moorabbin, Victoria, Australia: Hawker Brownlow Education, 2006).

[6] Nancy Chick, "What are Learning Styles?" Vanderbilt University Center for Teaching, Accessed 15 March 2020, https://cft.vanderbilt.edu/guides-sub-pages/ learning-styles-preferences/.

[7] Renate Nummela Caine and Geoffrey Caine, Making Connections: Teaching and the Human Brain, First Edition (Association for Supervision and Curriculum Development, 1991).

[8] James Garbarino, "Our Response to the Attack on America: What Can It Teach Children about Understanding and Revenge?" Child & Youth Care 19, no. 9, (September 2001).

[9] "40 Developmental Assets® for Adolescents (Ages 12–18)." 40 Developmental Assets® for Adolescents (Ages 12–18). Search Institute, n.d.

[10] The Developmental Assets Framework, Search Institute, https://www. search-institute.org/our-research/development-assets/developmental-assets-framework/.

[11] J. Luft and H. Ingham (1955), "The Johari window, a graphic model of interpersonal awareness," Proceedings of the Western Training Laboratory in Group Development. Los Angeles: University of California, Los Angeles.

[12] Eric Jensen, *The Engaging Classroom: Discipline Made Easy*,. The Brain Store, http://www.learninglandscape.com/The_Brain_Store_eBooklet.pdf .

[13] "Suspension / Expulsion Statistics," Colorado Department of Education, Updated November 19, 2019, https://www.cde.state.co.us/cdereval/suspend-expelcurrent

[14] Stephen Covey, *The 7 Habits of Highly Effective People: Powerful Lessons in Personal Change*, Anniversary Edition (Simon & Schuster, 2013).

[15] University of Rochester Medical Center, "Understanding the Teen Brain." University of Rochester Medical Center, Accessed March 15, 2020, https://www.urmc.rochester.edu/encyclopedia/content.aspx?ContentTypeID=1&ContentID=3051.

[16] Seth Chaiklin, "The Zone of Proximal Development in Vygotskys Analysis of Learning and Instruction," Vygotskys Educational Theory in Cultural Context, 2003, 39–64. https://doi.org/10.1017/cbo9780511840975.004.

[17] Lori Desautels, "Aiming for Discipline Instead of Punishment," Edutopia, March 1, 2008, https://www.edutopia.org/article/aiming-discipline-instead-punishment.

[18] Paul D. MacLean, *The Triune Brain in Evolution: Role in Paleocerebral Functions*, 1990 Edition (Springer, 1990).

[19] Sherrie Bourg Carter, "Emotions Are Contagious—Choose Your Company Wisely," *Psychology Today*, October 20, 2012, https://www.psychologytoday.com/us/blog/high-octane-women/201210/emotions-are-contagious-choose-your-company-wisely.

[20] Lally, Phillippa Lally, Cornelia H. M. van Jaarsveld, Henry W. W. Potts, and Jane Wardle, "How are Habits Formed: Miodelling Habit Formation in the Real World," *European Journal of Social Psychology*, July, 16, 2019, https://onlinelibrary.wiley.com/doi/abs/10.1002/ejsp.674.

[21] David A. Sousa, *How the Brain Learns*, Fifth Edition (Corwin, 2016).

Extend the Learning of Positive Behavior Principles

Concerned about losing momentum and focus as you work to integrate the principles into your daily routine? Consider using the ***Positive Behavior Principles Graphic Summary Posters*** for review.

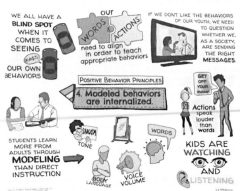

Each page has full-color pictures highlighting the main points from a principle to aid in retention.

The nine-sheet set come in two sizes – 8.5 x 11 card stock sheets for handy reference, or larger posters that can be used in faculty lounges.

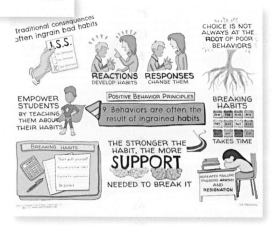

Available at
danstromain.com

Acknowledgements

As noted, the Positive Behavior Principles unfolded over time. They became evident and slowly evolved as my beliefs about behavior changed. Accordingly, I am thankful for all the people throughout my career who both directly and indirectly influenced the information in this book.

Working with and learning from Dr. Bruce Perry and Dr. Nicholas Long just after graduate school piqued my initial interest in human behavior—and shortly thereafter, I was exposed to the work of both Alfie Kohn and Dr. Martin Brokenleg, which was transformational.

When I started teaching, I was both encouraged and empowered by several of my supervisors, specifically Mary Lou Shuffler, Kris Holliday and Jacob Saucedo. They taught me to trust my instincts on what I knew could work if we moved beyond traditional discipline methods.

While working at the Region 20 Education Service Center in San Antonio, Texas, my colleague, Cindy Jones, and a whole host of amazing consultants, too numerous to name, continually fed my thirst for learning about educational best practices. The synergy created by these individuals was amazing.

Shout-outs also go to Dr. Elizabeth Salmeron, Eric Jenson, Dr. Jenny Severson, Jeannie Parsons, Dr. James Geidner, and my behavioral mentor and friend, Jo Mascorro — all of whom at some point had a profound impact on me, and in some way, this body of work.

Thanks to the National Center for Youth Issues, specifically the dynamic duo of Jennifer Deshler, my publisher, and Jennifer Gingerich, my editor, for helping this book come to fruition. I couldn't have written it without their input, encouragement, and support.

And finally, much love and thanks go to my amazing wife, boys, and life-long friends who continually stand beside me despite my own set of challenging behaviors.

Dan St. Romain

EDUCATIONAL CONSULTANT AND NATIONAL SPEAKER

Dan St. Romain is a national independent educational consultant, based out of San Antonio, Texas, who provides staff development and consultative services to educators and parents working with children of all ages. Dan is passionate about helping individuals shift their perspective on discipline, understanding the best ways to provide support given the challenges posed in today's society.

After receiving his master's degree in education, Dan worked in both private residential and public school settings. His work as a self-contained behavior unit teacher, Educational Diagnostician, Director of a Learning Resource Center, and behavior consultant afforded him experience at all levels, in both general and special education settings.

Dan's overwhelming strength is his skill as a presenter. Although his sessions are exceedingly interactive, his greatest asset lies in his ability to offer participants rich insight into the connectedness between educational practices and student behavior. Dan is the author of *Teach Skills and Break Habits: Growth Mindsets for Better Behavior in the Classroom*, and several resources for teaching social skills, featuring his Chameleon, Juan Pablo.

After having worked in the school system for the past thirty years, Dan has retired and is excited about this next phase in life. Although he will continue to offer staff development and write, Dan hopes to spend a great deal more time with his wife (also a retired teacher), gardening, and traveling.

Connect with Dan at:

www.danstromain.com • dan@danstromain.com • Twitter @danstromain

Popular Sessions Offered by Dan

KEYNOTES:

Mixed Messages: The Changing Face of Discipline

Toto, you're not in Kansas anymore! More and more, it seems like discipline issues are the main topic of conversation in the school setting. In this thought-provoking and interactive keynote session, participants examine the main influences impacting behavior over the last few decades and discuss implications for best practices as a result.

The Ripple Effect

When you throw a stone into a pond, sometimes it simply sinks—"plop." However, if thrown just right, the rock skips. Instead of the singular "plop", the skipping rock reaches more water, leaving ripples on the surface - and this energy changes the entire pond. As educators, we throw the stone. In this dynamic opening session, educators will learn simple ways we create ripples in the school setting that positively impact the students we serve.

Accentuate the Positive: Assets Students Need for Success

When we look at the long-term goals we have for students in the school system, they go way beyond the isolated short-term goal of passing a state mandated test. Research clearly indicates what youth need to be successful in school, as well as beyond. This interactive session will feature this information, as well as ways to encourage healthy development at all levels.

BREAKOUTS AND WORKSHOPS:

Positive Behavior Principles

Although behaviors in the school system have changed a great deal in the past few decades, our strategies for supporting those behaviors have not. By examining all the information we have learned about the brain, we are in a better position to design effective interventions. In this fast-paced session, participants will learn nine principles for positively shaping the behavior of our students.

Don't Go There: Avoiding Power Struggles

Even the most rational educators get into power struggles from time to time. In this active session, participants will gain a better understanding of how power struggles occur and learn the best strategies for avoiding them. This information is applicable at all levels and has implications for dealing with students and adults, alike.

I'm Bored: Engaging the Disengaged

"Is this going to be on the test?" "Do I have to do that?" Motivation and engagement are critical factors in helping our students find success in school. This session will feature simple ways to keep students actively plugged into teaching efforts. Participants will learn how to facilitate lessons that help students not only pay better attention in class, but also better retain the content being taught.

Teach Skills and Break Habits: Growth Mindsets for Better Behavior in the Classroom

How do we create long-term change for students with chronic behavior problems? In this session, attendees will discuss the downfall of common behavior tracking systems, as well as why time out, clip systems, behavior folders, and office referrals often work against our long-term goals. Participants will leave the session with ideas for both targeting and teaching skills, based on students' gifts and challenges.

I Can Make Good Choices

"You're so mean!" "You can't play with us!" "That's not fair!" Each year, educators are dealing with more behavior problems in the primary classrooms. In this interactive session, participants will learn quick and easy ideas for teaching behavioral skills using visuals, literature, chants and engaging activities.

You can have Dan speak at your next event!
Call **866.318.6294** or email **info@ncyi.org** for more details.

Other books from Dan St. Romain

TEACH SKILLS and BREAK HABITS

Growth Mindsets for Better Behavior in the Classroom

By Dan St. Romain

Good behavior is a skill that can be taught – and developed through practice. It just requires a shift in our perspective.

If you have tried behavior folders, clip systems, or other interventions based on punishments and rewards, you've probably discovered these one-size-fits-all approaches to behavior management all too often prove to be ineffective with the very students they were designed to help.

Teach Skills and Build Habits explores the reasons why what we've been doing isn't working, and how to find a new path and process that will lead to better behavior in the classroom, as well as success for students beyond their school years.

This book is for you if:
- You are an educator looking for help with student behaviors
- You spend more time managing behaviors than teaching
- Your current methods don't seem to be working
- You are looking for practical behavior strategies that can be used in a variety of settings

You will be empowered to:
- Focus on behavior change as a process of continual improvement
- Use behavior concerns as an opportunity to teach your students skills
- Help your students build on their gifts, accept their challenges, and practice areas of concern
- Build a foundation of good behavior in your students by establishing healthy relationships and creating a positive classroom climate

Dan's work in our division around his book *Teach Skills and Break Habits* helped our teachers shift their mindsets and philosophies to understand that poor behaviors are often a result of skill deficits and bad habits which have been learned. As a result, teachers have become more focused on effective ways to teach and practice skills rather than doling out rewards and consequences to change behaviors.

S. Cooper, Title I Coordinator
Virginia Beach, Virginia

Published by

Other resources from Dan St. Romain

Need some quick and easy methods for teaching social skills at the primary level? These resources were designed for teachers, counselors, administrators, and other mental health professionals working to shape the behavior of young children. Though not part of a specific program, the materials complement efforts based on the philosophy of using discipline as a teachable moment.

10 Simple Lessons for Better Behavior In The Classroom
10 More Simple Lessons for Better Behavior In The Classroom

You can teach a social skill in an isolated lesson, but the skill is most internalized when referenced during teachable moments. These short lessons feature simple concepts and consistent language, which provide teachers with an easy frame of reference to use when teaching students positive behaviors.

10 Simple Songs for Better Behavior In The Classroom
10 More Simple Songs for Better Behavior In The Classroom

Why repeatedly tell students what you want them to do when you can just sing your expectations? These spiralbound books and accompanying CDs feature songs that can be sung to familiar tunes to teach everyday social skills students need to find success at school and beyond.

How Are You Feelin', Juan Pablo Chameleon?

Do you have students who act out due to issues of hunger? Lack of sleep? Anger? This fun book features Juan Pablo Chameleon whose moods change as quickly as his colors. It can be used to teach children how to both identify and channel the most common feelings they experience on a daily basis.

Yummy, Yummy, In My Tummy

In school, teachers give students what they need to be successful, but they don't always give them what they want. The lesson of accepting disappointment appropriately can be difficult for some students. In this book, Juan Pablo is back with his best friend, Jax. Juan Pablo wakes up hungry and wants to eat everything in sight, but he soon learns a very important lesson: It's not always good to get everything you want.

Available at
danstromain.com

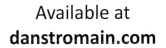

NATIONAL CENTER for
YOUTH ISSUES

About NCYI

National Center for Youth Issues provides educational resources, training, and support programs to foster the healthy social, emotional, and physical development of children and youth. Since our founding in 1981, NCYI has established a reputation as one of the country's leading providers of teaching materials and training for counseling and student-support professionals. NCYI helps meet the immediate needs of students throughout the nation by ensuring those who mentor them are well prepared to respond across the developmental spectrum.

Connect With Us Online!

@nationalcenterforyouthissues

@ncyi

@nationalcenterforyouthissues